THE BEST WORST THING THAT HAPPENED TO ME

Live in Gratitude!
Waleuska

Also by Waleuska Lazo:

The Gift of Bravery, The Story of Eli Cohen:
Our Hero and Spy

The Gift of Believing, The Story of Ben Carson:
Our Surgeon Extraordinaire

THE BEST WORST THING THAT HAPPENED TO ME

....

FROM VICTIM TO ARCHITECT OF MY LIFE

WALEUSKA LAZO

DREAMCATCHER PRINT

DreamCatcher Print/Waleuska Lazo
www.waleuskalazo.com

Copy Editing by Stephanie Gunning
Cover Design by Gus Yoo
Cover Photograph by Kathy Russel Photography, Florida
Book Layout ©2019 Book Design Templates

Ordering Information:
Quantity sales. Special discounts are available on quantity purchases by corporations, associations, reading groups, and others. For details, contact the publisher at the address above.

The Best Worst Thing That Happened to Me/Waleuska Lazo.
—1st ed.
ISBN 978-1-7327431-0-6

CONTENTS

DEDICATION

To my younger self

I humbly dedicate this book to you in gratitude for our brave journey and the resilient legacy we leave behind to those whom we've had the privilege to love.

Thank you for being vulnerable, brave, and courageous enough to hold my hand in the times of darkness and to walk with me through this miraculous thing we call life.

....

"The Universe has shaken you to awaken you."
—*Mastin Kipp*

On April 2, 2016, I had a nervous breakdown. The illusion of the world I'd manufactured in my mind was torn down, leaving me feeling naked and exposed to a reality that I had fought to hide for so long. During the healing and spiritual process that I engaged in after this, I learned three fundamental truths that have drastically changed and improved my life.

Why am I telling you this up front? Because as you read about the different moments of brightness and darkness in my polka-dot life, I want you to be able to appreciate these components of human existence at play in your own life.

The first truth may be difficult for you to accept. It was for me. But the sooner you understand it, the sooner you can start healing.

Here it comes.

First Truth

Everything you experience in your lifetime, good or bad, is created by you. God gave you this power. As the Bulgarian philosopher Omraam Mikhaël Aïvanhov wrote, "The creator has planted within every creature a fragment of himself, a spark, and a spirit of the same nature as himself and, thanks to this spirit; every creature can become a creator."[1]

The key words here are *every creature.* That means you and me. Both of us are responsible for the events, actions, and circumstances of our lives.

How is this possible?

We energetically create or attract whatever we think about: the good, the happy, the ugly, the painful, the love, the grief—everything in its totality. As beings of energy, our thoughts send vibrational waves of energy out into the quantum field of the universe, like signals; in turn, this field reflects our reality back to us.

You may object, saying, *"Wait a minute, I never wanted painful things in my life!"*

I understand. I said the same thing.

The fact is that on some unconscious level you did.

Everything I've learned about the power of the brain in the last few years suggests that we are not even aware of as much as 95 percent of the thoughts we think daily; *these thoughts are subconscious and conditioned.* We are so unaware of this programming that we need to be very careful about what we allow to take residence in our minds. Any time the mind gets stuck, the energy available to us to create and attract better experiences is limited.

> We energetically create or attract whatever we think about: the good, the happy, the ugly, the painful.

But wait. The situation gets worse. Not only do we attract things based on what we think about on a regular basis, sometimes what we attract is a fluke. According to Joe Dispenza, "You create by not creating. If you are not actively creating your life, you leave it to the randomness of reality and something is going to bump into you."[2]

Everything I have learned tells me that we are not simply bystanders in the world, or that things are happening independently of us. We are active participants in, and cocreators of, the world we live in.

We attract that which is on the same frequency as us. Conscious or not, willingly or not, things vibrating at the same level we are vibrating can be expected to come into our energy field and thus our lives. We need to learn to be more active creators because the human brain is mighty.

Once I understood that thoughts become things and that I was responsible fully for the outcomes of my life, I stopped blaming others to bail myself out and took responsibility for my actions and life. By shifting my perception, I went from being a victim to an empowered agent who capably steers and adjusts the sails of my boat on my journey through life.

Second Truth

Every painful event in your life holds a seed of enlightenment. If you choose to cultivate these seeds, you'll gain wisdom. Pain can be an excellent teacher.

Hurting sucks. Yes, it does. I do not know any human being who would willingly want to go through times of hardship. It is not in our nature to want to suffer, yet many of us spend our whole lives acting as if we're imprisoned with a faithful cellmate named misery.

Our fear of hurting is the reason why so many have a difficult time recognizing painful moments as opportunities to learn and evolve. We view our misfortunes as punishments rather than lessons we should be grateful for. But we can, as Gregg Braden says, "Change hurt into wisdom by finding new meaning in painful experiences."[3]

It is amazing, the strength you can derive from pain. Pain can either paralyze and victimize you or it can open you up and liberate you. When I understood this, I began to see painful experiences in my life as wise agents that have come to teach me something valuable, sometimes gently and sometimes harshly, but either way to sharpen and guide me closer to my goals and dreams. It was all a matter of changing the lens through which I looked at the pain.

I shifted my perception and rather than seeing painful experiences as something permanent, which is what we often do while engulfed in it, I thought of it as something temporary. This may sound simple or common sense to you—it actually is—but common sense isn't common. Learning to see the pain in your life as a teacher and as temporary can be one of the best strategies to become empowered. This way, you don't get to be a powerless victim any longer. You become a student who is wiser and grateful for the lessons.

Third Truth

You are not alone. The Universe (the term I use to describe a higher, divine intelligence) is forever on guard and guiding you in a proper direction through signs and nudges. It wants to help you find a path aligned with your soul purpose.

I hope this brings you comfort. Out of the three truths, the first and third were the most empowering for me. The fact that a cosmic power is guiding me was mainly comforting. Once I became aware of and receptive to it, I saw evidence of this everywhere and I was surprised to see how active a role the Universe plays in our lives.

The Universe does not just give
you what you want; it gives you
what you need.

The Universe does not just give you what you want; it gives you what you need. It will use any means necessary to get your attention, including loss, grief, death, sickness, and on many occasions, even the people you love. It finds ways to show you things you have hidden in the depths of your being that you need to remember, know, and act upon. It will bring to the surface of your conscious awareness all the things you need to address, learn, and heal so that ultimately you can reach your intended destiny.

This realization did not come quickly for me.

I am telling you this calmly now because I've already made peace with events in my life. But I can tell you that there was nothing peaceful or friendly about my initial encounters with the Universe. She came knocking at my door. My turn had come to learn karmic lessons, but I received her with mighty resistance.

I was a worthy opponent in a game of tug-o-war. The Universe pushed in one direction and I defiantly pulled in the other. The more she pulled, the harder I pulled. The more I struggled and resisted, the more painful her lessons became.

Who finally won, you may ask? She did. I am happy and grateful to say the Universe got the upper hand on me at last. And with this I recognized that it was time to quit fighting.

My point is this. You can trust the Universe, even if you can't see or understand her plan. She knows what she is doing. For me, it was in those thorny experiences of pulling with bleeding hands on the rope of enlightenment that I learned the most profound lessons of my existence. I now humbly share these with you.

ONE

ROOTS AND WINGS

*"Fear and faith have something in common. They both ask us
to believe in something we cannot see."*
—Joel Osteen

I was born in Corinto, a Colonial Spanish port town located on the northwest coast of Nicaragua in Central America. My beautiful Corinto, which is surrounded by the warm waters of the Pacific Ocean, is a true fisherman's town that moves slowly to the rhythm of its boats, cargo ships, and legends. The main commerce when I was growing up there in the 1970s revolved around the import and export of goods arriving on ships from all over the world, such as oil, cereals, automotive equipment, and fertilizer.

In Corinto everything was close, but my family's home was situated within walking distance to all the main attractions. Just a few blocks away were the shipping docks. I can remember as a child watching hundreds of cargo trucks line up by the port for the loading or unloading of merchandise. Goods were lifted into the air by cranes inside massive metal containers containing exports from Nicaragua, such as coffee, cotton, rum, methanol, and other agricultural products, that were to be shipped to Europe and Asia, as well as neighboring Latin American countries.

I grew up in the home of my grandmother, whom I affectionately called Mama Rosita, a home full of love. Like many Spanish families, my entire family lived together under one roof. I grew up with my parents, my aunts Patricia and Rialuga, my uncle Marcos, and my nanny, Maria Isabel, who were the youngest people in the household. The older ones were Mama Rosita, my great-grandmother Candida, my great aunts Chepita and Lula, whom we all affectionately called Mama Lula, my great uncle Toño, and other seniors who would come to stay with us for weeks at a time throughout the year. When I say *seniors*, I am talking about an age range spanning from the 80s to the 90s and beyond—all the way to age 104.

As far back as I can remember, these relations and family friends were already old. I kid you not, our home seemed more like a nursing home than a regular home. If you ever watched the movie *Cocoon* (1985), which was a science fiction story about a group of seniors in a retirement home, then you can imagine what I am talking about. Yes, that was my home! It was a funny place to live, but I would not change it for the world.

I had the good fortune to be raised by three strong, courageous women.

I had the good fortune to be raised by three strong, guerrilla women: my mother, Magda; Mama Rosita, and my unforgettable great grandmother, Candida. These three women embodied strength, resilience, courage, and love for their family, and they were also excellent examples of entrepreneurship at its best.

Mama Rosita, who was widowed when she was still very young, had needed to raise her five children completely on her own. An obstetrician by trade, she was well known all over the port. Word had it that she helped deliver the children in half the families in the community. An amazing businesswoman, she was not afraid to do whatever she needed to do to make sure that all her children would get the education they needed to become professionals.

Great Grandmother Candida helped support the household. She was a fierce saleswoman. Along with helping raise my father and uncles, she sold used clothing and shoes and served the people of Corinto as a money lender.

My young mother worked long hours in the shipping dock offices, *la Portuaria,* as a data entry clerk, while my father attended medical school. Because of their career ambitions, my parents sacrificed their time with me. I spent most of my early years with my nanny and the members of my *Cocoon* family. Some of my best memories of childhood are of playing all kinds of tricks on them. I was vicious. I would hide their canes, tied cords to their wheelchairs so they could not move, and switched their shoes so they would wear them reversed or wore different shoes on each foot. I loved playing jokes on them. I would spend my days scheming about ways to spook them at night. Since the old people believed in ghosts, scaring them turned into a fascination for me and I was gifted at it.

When I think back to my childhood, the image that comes to mind most quickly is seeing the old people seated in a straight line on their rocking chairs, where they slept most of the day.

I used to laugh a lot seeing how they fought and prayed. It was hilarious! They would be praying one minute, and then the next I would hear my great grandma Candida tell my great aunt Chepita that she was the devil incarnate. These fights, which were so entertaining, would begin and end for no apparent reason. After a flareup, as if nothing had happened, the old folks would all go back to either praying or sleeping.

There was never a dull moment in the house. My great uncle Toño, who lived to eat, was constantly choking, so everyone would have to run to the rescue. While one adult would hit his back, another would hit his chest, and someone else would pull his arms up to get air to move into his lungs. The display was hysterical, and it happened at least once a day.

Another fond memory is of hiding in the backyard behind the trees to watch Great Aunt Chepita chase the chickens. I would laugh at the fact that she talked out loud to herself and the chickens all day long. If one pecked her, watch out! She would take the chicken by the throat, twist it a couple of rounds, put it in a boiling pot of hot water, then unfeather the poor thing. Guess what was for dinner that night? You got it!

I do not want to give you the impression that I did not respect the seniors, because I did. I was just young and mischievous. I meant no harm. I loved my *Cocoon* family and I could never envision my life without them. I delighted sitting for hours on their laps to hear all about their life experiences and the amazing folk stories and urban legends they knew about ghosts, apparitions, and hauntings.

There was never a dull moment in the house.

Like many ancient cultures, in Spanish culture knowledge is passed down orally. The elderly pass along their knowledge to their descendants through storytelling, and my family were amazing storytellers. They were my greatest sources of entertainment and my greatest teachers.

During the days when I was not in school, I spent a great deal of time playing on the streets. Back in the day, that was the normal thing to do. It was safe and everyone in the community knew who I was. There were no cell phones, so the street lights turning on was the cue reminding my friends and I that we needed to head home.

There was a railway station about fifty meters to the south of our humble home. Playing on the train tracks near the station was the highlight of my day. I enjoyed climbing between the empty cabins of the trains that were being stationed overnight. I would daydream that I was taking the Orient Express to explore exotic lands.

South of the house and across from the station, there also was an ice cream parlor where I would partake in tasting many of the flavors several times a day. The owners lived next door to my family, and apparently when I was two I would cry late at nights demanding Popsicles. My screams were so severe that the owners would rush to pass a Popsicle over the backyard fence to shut me up.

The town's beautiful central park, Parque José Santos Zelaya, was located only a block from my home. It had a pink clock tower and a bronze cannon, and I have a lot of happy childhood memories of playing there.

I have a lot of happy childhood memories.

The church was diagonal to the railway station and the market not far down the street from it. I loved going to the outdoor market and walking the streets packed with food vendors who had placed massive wicker baskets full of fresh vegetables and fruits on the ground. I was sure always to return home with my hands full of goodies.

Our next-door neighbors on the north side of the house, were a Chinese family who owned a restaurant called El Muchong. I was friends with the grandchildren.

They made the best Chinese food ever, especially their noodle soups. My God! What I would give to have one of those soups right now.

I remember going over during the day and sitting right next to don Benjamin, the patriarch of the family, and watching him make the noodles from scratch. He sat at a very long wooden table with a metal machine on it that to me seemed like a presser—much like the machines that press bedroom sheets. He used to feed long sheets of dough through this device, which would come out the other end pressed flat; and then he would put them through another machine that would turn the flat sheets into long, perfectly cut, delicious noodles. He would then hang the noodles to dry.

Don Benjamin was not much for words. I honestly don't even think he spoke much Spanish. I only remember him speaking the same few words to me. But he would hum all day as he worked on his noodles—a Chinese melody so soft that to me it sounded like heavenly harmonies. I was fascinated.

After El Muchong, there was the cinema, El Cine Mercedes. I told you my house was amazingly situated, didn't I? Right in front of this theater, there were all kinds of street vendors selling food. After dinner I used to ride my tricycle to buy plantain chips or ready-to-eat slices of green mango in a plastic bag with salt. Oh my god!

Now I see why I crave noodle soups, plantain chips, and salty things, such as the green mangos I ate as a child, when I am feeling stressed or sad. I never made the connection until I started telling you just now about my childhood. It is clear to me that these foods are ingrained in my subconscious as sources of the comfort I felt when I was young.

And who can forget the taco stand with its steaming hot tacos produced in huge greasy pans of bubbling oil and served with creamy coleslaw? Yes, those were the good old days!

We did not spend our nights back then watching TV as people do nowadays. Nights were spent sitting on the porch in wooden rocking chairs. We would all sit together and watch the people going to the movies pass by. Every moment someone else would stop to talk to my family. I remember the sound of laughter and a camaraderie that I have never seen in North America. People were not rich in Corinto, but they were happy. At least that is what my childhood senses perceived them as being.

I don't know why it was, but Mama Rosita's house was always full of people. She apparently could never say no to anyone in need. *"If there is food for one, there is food for all,"* she would say. Not a day went by that someone did not come to visit. Some, instead of coming for the day, would stay a couple of weeks at a time.

One of our daily guests was Doña Clarisa who had been friends with Mama Rosita since they were in high school together.

The most repeated guest was an unusual blond woman covered from head to toe in freckles, Yvonne Giboulet. She looked German to me, as she was extremely fair, which for Nicaragua is unusual. I later learned she was of French descent. I believe one of her teenage sons, Jimmy, who was a few years younger than my dad, was a runaway living on the streets and shining shoes to get by. My uncle Mauricio, my dad's brother, brought him home one day. He too became a permanent resident. That must have been how Yvonne came to be in Mama Rosita's life.

When Jimmy was older, he became a sailor and left in a ship. Whenever the ship came to port, he always paid his gratitude to his second mother, who took him from the streets.

Yvonne was a difficult woman. That must be why Jimmy ran away. I found her interesting. She would sit all day in a rocking chair, and as far as I can remember she always had a cigarette in her mouth. God knows how many packs a day she smoked. I guess back in the 1970s people were oblivious to the causes of lung cancer.

Yvonne also had a filthy mouth on her. Nicaraguans are notorious for having toilet mouths, but she was the queen of them all. There was no sentence she spoke that did not contain at least a few profanities. To her, it was natural. To me, it was hilarious.

Even though Yvonne was always at our home, she never participated in the prayer group that Mama Rosita led. She probably figured that she would have to stop swearing if she did and that would cause her to go mute as so many of the words in her vocabulary would have needed to be censored.

Jimmy was not the only young person that Mama Rosita rescued. She put a few stray kids through school. Several adults that came to the house when I was little treated Mama Rosita as if she was their mother. They had been rescued by her when they were young, and many of them were now good income-producing citizens—professionals.

Mama Rosita was like a fairy godmother. Although she had no husband and had to work hard because she had many mouths to feed, she never stopped doing what her heart told her to do, which was to help people. Mama

Rosita took the little she had and, somehow, God multiplied it. There was always enough for all of us to eat, live, and be happy in her home.

Mama Rosita succeeded in putting four of her five children through university. My dad became a cardiologist. My aunt Edelweiss became a renowned ophthalmologist. My uncle Marcos studied law. My aunt Patricia studied biology. My poor uncle Mauricio died, but I am sure if he had lived, he too would have gone on to higher studies and become something great.

Why do I mention this? I find it admirable and courageous that Mama Rosita alone not only managed to raise great professionals, but as if the hardships of sole parenting weren't enough, she honored God by helping others in greater need than her kids.

I grew up sustained by the sweet smells of freshly brewed coffee with hot milk, creamy oatmeal with cinnamon, and the religious chants of Mama Rosita's weekly prayer group. Several times a week, she and fifteen or so of her friends would gather to read the Bible and give thanks to the Lord. The songs they sang were amazing. At three or four years old, I can remember sitting with them, chanting and raising my arms to the benevolent Universe. This was how I ordinarily spent the early years of my life. Perhaps it will not come as a surprise to you that this is the reason why, very early on, I developed an affinity for a higher presence.

Of course, I did not fully understand the true scope of my spirituality or realize that my beliefs would later evolve into a full-blown faith.

> Everything that has happened, is happening, or will happen only happens if that is the intention of God.

Mama Rosita taught me that nothing happens if is not the will of God. In other words: Everything that has happened, is happening, or will happen only happens if that is the intention of God. Furthermore, since God is love, then all things, even painful things, are happening to lead us to the path of our highest and greatest good.

Even when things were difficult for my grandmother, she would tell me that she had faith. That God would bring her out of any situation. This was the same woman who had lost a son to a horrific car accident when he was only sixteen years, had lost her husband, and was carrying huge responsibilities on her shoulders by agreeing to support the many people relying on her. Her faith was unshakable. And commendable.

She understood that whatever she and her family were going through, God put it there because it was what we needed to confront to learn something important.

I was taught always to look for the silver lining in things.

"When one door closes, somewhere God opens a window."

"God always provides,"

"The Lord is my shepherd, I shall not want."

"If God is with me, who can be against me?"

These are just a few of the mantras repeated throughout the day in my home when I was a child. When you grow up constantly hearing those phrases throughout your days and life, it is difficult to grow up without some sense of faith. Mama Rosita always said, "Believe even when there is no reason to believe."

I honestly do not know when exactly I began to deviate from this belief. Somewhere along the way, I forgot her teachings and my spirituality. I let the rational left side of my brain completely take over my thinking. The brain's left hemisphere controls our analytical and objective thinking. It controls our ability to create language and our movements. By contrast, the brain's right hemisphere is more emotional. It controls spirituality, intuition, creativity, and imagination.

Since I was a child, I always had a clear idea of the type of life I wanted to have as an adult. I studied. I was disciplined. I made goals for myself. I took calculated risks for my life. I had a happy life in Nicaragua. I had no complaints. But I felt that I needed more.

The political landscape was changing in my country. For forty-three years, Nicaragua was ruled by a dictatorship under the regime of the Somoza family. After the Nicaraguan Revolution in 1979, the Sandinista National Liberation Front (FSLN) established a communist regime in Nicaragua. But the political situation in my country did not get better. The economic disparity in Nicaragua was extremely noticeable and many complained about abuse and repression. My Nicaragua was forever changed.

Shortly after turning eight, I moved with my parents to Leon. Being from a middle-class family of professionals residing in Leon, the second most important city in Nicaragua, we were not witness to the worst of the unjust treatment of the Somoza family. The people in rural areas of the nation were looking for a better and more just government. When the FSLN took power, many were hopeful that for the first time in Nicaraguan history there would be equality and a better life for all.

Those hopes were short lived.

While some changes were implemented to assist the poor, no major shift toward equality was achieved.

Everything the FSLN said that they stood for in the moment of their victory was forgotten just a few years later. At the beginning, there was a big push made to educate everyone in the countryside who in the past had no access to basic education. The so-called *alphabetization* of the masses, in my opinion, was a positive policy the Sandinistas implemented. Many believed that it was by design that the Somoza regime had offered so little public education; it was a strategy to keep the masses controlled. Less educated people pose less of a threat to the status quo.

To bridge the gap between affluent and poor, after the Revolution there was some redistribution of land taken from the rich elite to the peasantry, which subsequently was owned in community (*coperativas*), but most of the wealth the FSLN confiscated was distributed among the new government officials. Ironically, they ended up doing all the corrupt things they had promised the people they would eliminate. They became just as wealthy, unjust, and repressive as members of the Somoza government, if not more.

The country became poorer than it was. If food was not available to everybody due to the poor not having the economic means to obtain it, now it was even scarcer because it did not matter if you had money, there simply was no food to buy. Most of the imports of food, cars, and manufactured goods came to a halt. The United States placed an embargo on Nicaragua in the early 1980s, just like it had embargoed Cuba.

Prior to the Revolution, much like in North America, Nicaraguans had everything to choose from in their local supermarkets. The FSLN nationalized shopping and closed the markets down. Then they instituted food rations through local CDS outlets. CDS stood for *Comités de Defensa de Sandinista.* Each family was given a ration card and, based on the number of people in a family, it was determined the amount of food you could obtain. There was never enough for our household. We got a ration of two bars of soap to wash our clothing every two weeks, a pound of sugar, two cases of eggs, and four rolls of toilet paper.

Nicaragua's main allies were Cuba and the Soviet Union and our country, unfortunately, became nothing more than a replica of the two. Most of the money was spent in obtaining weapons to fight the war against the Contras. A compulsory military service was established. The young generation were brainwashed so that many turned against their parents. All industries were nationalized. And education, even in the private schools, was controlled and delivered as the main means for control, propaganda, and indoctrination.

The wealthy were the enemy and the Sandinistas made no attempt to hide it. I was attending a private school, so I was constantly bullied on the streets and taunted by screams of "Bourgeoisie, leave."

In Nicaragua of that era, it was not uncommon to see your friends one day and then never see them again. People would disappear if the government believed they supported the opposition. The lucky ones who were rounded up made it out with a beating or a prison term. The unlucky ones are still missing to this day.

The Sandinistas had an extremely paranoid government. The revolutionaries would reward anyone with information or suspicion on anyone they felt opposed them. The people were watched constantly. Each community appointed a family that the FSLN knew were sympathizers whose role was to watch and report any activity that they saw in the neighborhood that they thought could be against the government.

There was no freedom of speech or movement. There was a curfew and if anyone was found roaming the streets past that established time, you had to deal with consequences.

My father, a well-known doctor, was appointed to be the chief forensic doctor in Leon and Chinandega. Part of his responsibilities was to oversee the health of political prisoners. My father who had never sympathized with the Somoza government was hopeful at the beginning of the Revolution. He had heard about all the social changes the new revolutionary government promised to make. However, he quickly saw that these were not the case and we were headed to the same level of repression and inequality, if not worse conditions. He began to forge medical reports and arrange for political prisoners to be taken out of the prisons for treatment, as well as arranging for many of them to escape.

You can imagine the danger in this. Yet my father was not able to just sit back and see the terrible abuse given to these people for the simple reason of disagreeing with the new regime.

One morning, my father received an anonymous call telling him to take his family and leave the city of Leon, where we were living at the time. I must have been ten at the time. We packed a bag and returned to Corinto, where my grandma lived. The next day at 2:30 p.m. we received information that our home had been burned to the ground. We had lost everything we had. I still remember going back to find only devastation, charred wood, and a crater in the ground where our home once stood. A bomb had taken out our house and the entire neighborhood.

A scene from a Hollywood movie, right?

Not for us. Not for many Nicaraguans.

For this and many other reasons, the lives of our family were in danger. By this time my three younger brothers had been born and my father was worrying about our future in a country that he clearly no longer recognized. I don't want to go into too much detail about the Revolution because it is not the intent for this book, but I could write one on the veil of illusion that communist regimes create to obtain and maintain control. Let me just tell you that each day we stayed there was one day less we could have been alive.

Months later, my father was being pressured to join the ranks of the government. When he declined, my three younger brothers did not make it home at their usual time from school and none of their friends knew where they were.

Yes, your guess is correct. They had been taken.

After three days of my brothers being missing, they were finally released in a rural road after being interrogated at their young age of seven, six, and four years about the activities and opinions of my father toward the Revolution.

There was no question. We had to leave our homeland if we were to have any hope of a normal life.

Depending on where you come from, the simple pursuit of personal safety is something that may be foreign to you. Growing up in Nicaragua, life was different than it is in North America. I would be riding my bike on the streets one moment, and the next moment I would be running to a shelter because bullets were flying on the streets.

Since there were no diplomatic ties and no friendship with the United States at the time, it was very difficult to obtain a visa from the U.S. consulate. Just so you can get an idea, if 500 people went there to obtain a visa, maybe 15 of them received one. For males aged 14 to 46, it was the law that you could not leave the country due to compulsory military service, so my brothers and father had to stay. My mother and I, however, were among the lucky ones to obtain one-year permits to go visit the Land of Opportunity, the Land of the Free!

To make a long story short, I am happy to tell you that my father managed at a great risk to escape with my three brothers eight months later and the family reunited in Miami.

God works in miraculous ways. My father was invited to attend a medical convention in Guatemala for cardiology and he asked the Nicaraguan government for permission to go. He was granted a two-week pass and escorted to the plane. What the government did not know is that my three brothers had boarded an earlier flight. Once in Guatemala, they never left the airport. They proceeded to take a flight to Miami.

Immediately upon arriving, U.S. custom officials wanted to arrest them and deport them back to Nicaragua. Thankfully by this time, however, the political situation in Nicaragua was so public around the world and human rights violation was at the front page of every major newspaper in the world. Canada took them in.

Canada. Wow! I am getting teary eyed as I write this. Canada was the only country who had an open-door policy for Nicaraguans being politically persecuted. My father relentlessly told U.S. immigration that our lives were in danger and that we did not mean to violate their laws; we were simply in transit to Canada under the Migration and Refugee Assistance Act. After two days of being detained at the Miami Airport, we boarded a plane to Canada, leaving our troubles behind.

TWO

······································

A NEW START IN A NEW LAND

"The struggle is part of the story."
—Alina Ernilova

In pursuit of a better and safer life, on July 11, 1987, my family arrived in Canada, claiming political asylum. Canada has been my home ever since. Although it was sad to leave my motherland, every sacrifice made was well worth it. Today, decades later, my children, like everyone else in North America, are free to speak their minds without repression. When they reach maturity, they'll be entitled to vote and their vote will make a difference. They can walk the streets in safety without curfews, and they can pursue their dreams with no limitations. We were privileged to be welcomed.

Still, life in Canada was not easy initially. We arrived with nothing but a dream. The only person we knew was a cousin of my father who helped orient us; otherwise we were at the mercy of our surroundings and had to rely on our own wits. Without money or social connections, and worse, without being able to speak and read English, the first three years tested us.

Until we learned proper English, my mother and I worked in a factory, folding sweaters. My parents obtained modest financial assistance from the government that enabled them to pay for a small rental apartment, really an attic, in a haunted house on Weston Road in the west end of Toronto. We could not afford fans and air conditioning was a luxury we didn't even dare dream of, so it was very hot in our home during the summer. Our wardrobes for the first few years came from the Goodwill or Salvation Army second-hand stores.

To purchase enough food for six mouths, including the mouths of three growing boys, we supplemented our very low income with food stamps from various amazing organizations such as the Scott Mission on Spadina Avenue. We could not afford real meat or potatoes, so we made mashed potatoes from a powder that came in a box and ate soybean burgers. Boxes of macaroni cost

30 cents on sale at our local No Frills Supermarket, so this became a staple in our household.

Honestly, I do not know how my poor mother did it; she cooked with such love, I guess, that she ensured our meals were always tasty and filling. She was creative with the little we had. She would cook chicken wings, the only parts of the chicken that we could afford, with sliced tomatoes, onions, and herbs that made the meal taste like food intended for the gods.

As I write this, I find myself flooded with such gratitude for my mother and her efforts to make sure that her children never knew just how difficult things were for our family at that time. She did a remarkable job caring for us during the difficult period of transition. But although she ensured that we successfully endured the hardship of starting over from scratch, this was not the life I had envisioned for myself. I wanted more.

Living in rough conditions ignited a desire in me to get more, be more, and have more. I swore that I was never going to be poor again. Driven, I worked every day after school and on weekends to put myself through university, and after earning a four-year bachelor's degree, I enrolled in a master's program in criminal justice at the University of Toronto. On my own, I began to study leadership and success principles and applied what I was reading about to my life. I was enormously invested in the prospect of being able to control my life circumstances.

Of course, this is not surprising. After all, it is the immigrant mentality. Our parents always taught me and my siblings, "If you study hard and work hard, you will get the job of your dreams and success will come." And like them, I believed this was the recipe for happiness. It's why I became the decisive, ambitious, motivated, and tenacious woman I am today.

Everything seemed perfect.

In 1996, I graduated with honors and founded my first company, Embanet, an ed-tech service company, with the man I married that year. My husband, Jeffrey, and I were determined to bring education to people for whom it had formerly been out of reach. Life looked bright. I became a mother in 2002 and gave birth again in 2007. Everything seemed perfect. I was "living the dream," as people say. With amazing children, a thriving business, and a loving husband, I felt I had a great handle on my life and where I was going. I resonated with the popular saying "The harder I work, the luckier I get."

From age 17 to age 44, I lived according to the philosophy that the more I could control my environment, the better and safer I would be. And why not? All the self-help authors I read made some version of this point: Napoleon Hill, Brian Tracey, Robert T. Kiyosaki, Vince Lombardi, Og Mandingo, Dale Carnegie, Tony Robbins, Peter Sage, and Sun Tzu explicitly taught that I could control my destiny. And my experiences backed them up. I set goals for myself, and then achieved the outcome, based on my efforts alone.

> Life does not play favorites, it gives you exactly what you ask of it.

I have never been shy about asking life exactly what I want from it. My father used to say: Life does not play favorites, it gives you exactly what you ask of it. So, I asked a lot. I studied hard, worked hard, and set my goals high. I set daily, weekly, and yearly goals. I took courses in leadership, and mapped my life for the next five, ten, and twenty years. I even wrote my obituary and made detailed provisions for my departure from the world. I stipulated everything down to whom my pallbearers would be. And I described a plan B in case one or two of the pallbearer I wanted were unable to comply with my request. I hated the thought of being dead and having someone I didn't like carrying my coffin.

Does this sound like control issues to you, or what? Crazy, huh?

I wanted to control everything in my life and in death, I guess.

I have always considered myself a seeker. I believe in angels, spirit guides, and the manifestation of miracles. Believing for me has always been easy because I was never stuck on titles or names; nor did I care about the differences between religions. To this day, I do not care what name you use: Source, God, Jesus, Allah, Adonai, the Field, the Matrix, the Universe, or something else. Regardless of what you call it, I believe there is a higher intelligence in our lives. But as strong as my belief in a higher force was in principle, in action for many years I was too busy controlling things to request guidance or support, too busy living in a state of doing.

For me, life seemed to be a continuous race. Always striving for more: being the best student, getting into the best graduate program, finding the right partner, landing the most prestigious job, buying a big house or a great car, making the right friends, and, well, I don't need to go on as you can probably guess the rest of the list yourself. Pursuing these sorts of things can put you on a very narrow path, especially if you are a type A personality, like me.

You go through life completely unaware of the beauty around you, never seeing the things that truly matter. By the time you finally stop to catch your breath and look back, you realize that all that *doing* was for nothing, that its value was an illusion, and that you have, in fact, not lived at all.

That's tragic.

....

THREE

A TWISTED TURN OF EVENTS

Sometimes you must experience a low point in life to learn a lesson you wouldn't have learned any other way.

My husband and I worked night and day to build our business for 15 years. We left home before light and returned home after dark. Early on, while our friends were collecting nice paychecks at their corporate jobs, buying their first homes, and taking trips, Jeffrey and I bootstrapped it. The first year of our marriage we ate at his parents' house every night to save money. Because our business involved supporting online learners all over the world with their technical issues, our job required us to be present 24 hours, 7 days a week, 365 days a year.

The days were long and the tears many, but we persisted, and I am proud to say the effort paid off. Our company grew from being just the two of us working out of our bedroom to the two of us plus 365 full-time employees and another 300 contract facilitators, graphic designers, instructional designers, course content providers, and others, working in a 52,000-square-foot office. As pioneers in the online distance-learning community we achieved something special in our field. However, nothing comes from nothing. Our huge sacrifices took a toll on our marriage.

I felt hollow.

In 2007, Embanet was purchased by the American company Knowledge Universe. The deal was good. But just like that, in a matter of months, the thing that had been the central focus of my life for so long, besides caring for my daughter, Victoria, was gone. Feeling purposeless, I went into withdrawal.

Between 2010 and 2013, despite the arrival of my beloved second daughter, Emma, I went from living as if I was on top of the world and feeling I had a perfect life to feeling extremely unhappy with my life. How does a person make such a drastic change? In my case, a crazy desire to control everything ultimately led me to become someone I did not recognize. I looked in the mirror and the reflection I saw there did not match what I felt like inside. Inside, I felt hollow. Because I felt so empty emotionally, I was always looking to fill myself up with food or the next thing that might give me pleasure. I was having a difficult time losing my pregnancy weight, so I began dieting to control my weight. I was always chasing the achievement of a certain look or a certain weight, then reaching my goal and still feeling what in my delirious mind was "fat" and dissatisfied. Basically, I was always looking to the next goal or for another source of gratification yet feeling unfulfilled. Nothing was ever enough.

> I was always looking for another
> source of gratification.

Always looking for higher, for more, for better, it was like an addiction—I needed increasingly more of whatever I pursued to get the same effect. All the chasing of gratification was me racing against the clock of perfectionism as it ticked away my dignity, my peace, my self-love, and my hope. Despite having achieved much in my life, I rarely stopped to be grateful for what I had. I was too focused on the things that I thought I lacked.

This was a horrible way to live. Believe me.

More than once, people who cared about me asked, "Why aren't you ever happy? You always say that when you get X you'll be happy, but even though you get it you still aren't happy." I thought that they were crazy, and I felt insulted by this remark. But they were right. I was never happy. The emotional charge that I would get when they brought that to my attention was an indicator that they were triggering some truth at my core that needed to be healed.

I was out of touch with my soul. Despite being blessed in many areas of my life there was an element of anxiety and restlessness in me. Something profoundly needed was missing. This emptiness led me to hold on to things that were damaging. I fought for circumstances and people that, in the end, were not right for me. I was operating under the premise: "If I work hard enough at anything, if I keep trying, and if I never give up I can conquer anything." I was stubborn.

In 2013, my marriage ended. Soon afterward, I started dating – perhaps too soon. I was in denial of the pain I felt from having left Jeffrey, a man whom I deeply loved and trusted, but from whom I had grown apart, and I was desperate to numb the void.

As I mentioned earlier, the Universe will use any means possible to awaken us, including our intimate relationships. At the time, I was terrified of being alone. In hindsight, I can see I was avoiding feeling the pain that would come from giving awareness to my actions. What better way to numb my heart than with a rebound relationship, right? Then I met a man who would break my heart in the most painful way that any person can be hurt. I jumped into a relationship with him with both feet and ignored the warning signs, ignored my gut instincts that he was not the right man for me and basically acted like a spoiled little girl who wanted her way at any cost.

From the very start of this new relationship, the Universe sent me repeated signs and messages alerting me to issues that needed healing in me, which you, as an outsider, would have seen as clear as the best crystal. The relationship was so toxic it was destined to send me off a cliff emotionally. Yet I proceeded with full force— as I had many times before in other areas of my life— trying to obtain that which my heart desired. I thought that if I put in enough effort, I could fix it. They say there is no one so blind as someone who does not want to see. That was me!

The result? I wasted my precious time and my health began to suffer.

The big question is: Why was I so stubborn and fixated on this relationship? *Because I was so empty inside.* In a matter of seven years, my world had taken a different turn. Having sold my business, despite walking away with a tidy profit and loving my kids, I had no vision of where my life was headed anymore. I felt so empty and without a purpose that I frequently questioned my very existence. I kept asking myself, "What is my calling?"

"Why am I here?"

"What am I good at?"

"What is my gift?"

"Maybe I don't have any real gifts to offer the world."

"Am I just existing to exist?"

Knowing myself, I was never going to be satisfied with simply existing. I felt hungry to share something, to do something to change the world for the better. But how? Was my function to just be a mother and a wife, or did the Universe have something more to ask of me?

Because I couldn't answer these questions, seemingly no matter what I did, no matter what I achieved, no matter who I was with, nothing was ever enough. Worse, I blamed those I loved for my unhappiness. I became negative. I doubted my abilities. I was so focused on the things I felt I lacked that I was oblivious to, and unappreciative of, what the Universe had already bestowed upon me.

Please understand. Although I was feeling all those things, I had no grasp of the lessons the Universe was giving me. We're talking about a time before I learned how to ignite my divine cosmic essence. I had no psychological or spiritual tools to bring myself out of the darkness, and my faith muscle was dormant. I had no real sense of my days, my weeks, or my years.

I felt passionless, like a character in a play.

William Shakespeare wrote:

All the world's a stage,

And all the men and women, merely players …

Had my human existence been reduced to just being a player? And if I was a player in a play called life, who was the director? Whose play was I acting? Often, I felt that I was not even an actor but a spectator on the sidelines. My every outlook and state of mind was negative.

If you are on a spiritual path yourself, you probably already know that how we think and how we feel creates our state of being. Human beings can exist in two modes. Either we are in the mode of creation, growth, and possibility or we are in an emergency mode, where we are shutting down and contracting. We cannot exist in both modes simultaneously.

I was stagnating because I'd stopped doing things that had formerly inspired me. I was not evolving in any sense of the word. And after my relationship failed miserably, I was in full-blown survival mode and controlled by stress hormones; thus, my ability to contemplate internal change, which was what I urgently needed to do, was not possible. If your mind perceives that you are in danger it does what is designed to do: It keeps you safe in the known.

There are no shortcuts in life, sooner or later you need to pay the toll.

Change requires work. By facing our painful experiences and fears we can gain the wisdom we need to become who we are meant to be. I love Glennon Doyle Melton's comment: "To transform, we need to face the grief, the loneliness of now. If we ease our way out of pain, we are like a caterpillar that jumps out of the cocoon right before we become a butterfly."[1]

Sad to say, I took the road that I thought was going to take me directly to a life of bliss. Instead, it led me into a hellish abyss. On this dark and twisted road, I tried many times to turn back, but I became lost; each way I turned I ran into a new dead end, and I could not find my way home to myself. Signs are everywhere if we choose to see them. I guess I knew that, but I'd become anesthetized, blind, and conditioned to seeing only what I conveniently wanted to see. I chose the road I thought was easier and would enable me to avoid paying tolls. Unfortunately, I learned that there are no shortcuts in life and sooner or later you need to pay the toll.

In retrospect, I think I was too scared to acknowledge the signs because if I did, it would mean I had to act on them and I simply did not want to yet. It was easier for me to ignore the Universe who graciously respected my free will to choose my path for myself.

Thankfully, the Universe never gives up on us. She is always there waiting for us to open our hearts and minds. Like a good parent, the Universe maintains a perfect balance of respecting our free will and never leaving us completely alone. The Universe tries to help us find peace. As Marianne Williamson says, "The Universe works like a GPS. Even if a wrong turn gets taken on the way to your destination, the GPS will simply recalibrate and provide another route."[2]

Now, depending on how stubborn you are, it may take the Universe many attempts to get through to you about what your best interests are. This was the case with me. I kept postponing seeing the obvious signs and so the warnings went from gentle nudges to loud alarm bells.

If you ever do what I did, rest assured that until you finally choose to wake up, the Universe will never stop sending you messages disguised as necessary to reach you—and send them with increasing intensity. In his book *Moments Matter,* businessman John Goodman describes this phenomenon. "It's amazing how the Universe turns up the volume. If we don't get the message the first time, it will reappear in a different form and at a higher volume."[3] Every situation in our lives is a mirror reflecting our behavior back to us. Every relationship is a mirror of our conscious and unconscious motivations, desires, intentions, decisions, and choices.

You may be able to postpone a lesson, but never to escape it.

The Universe is relentless. She will use any method at her disposal, throwing you into similar or worse situations until you finally see what the mirrors are revealing and learn the lessons you are intended to learn. You may be able to postpone a lesson, but never to escape it.

Now I laugh at the Universe's persistence. I know it's best not to fight her. There is no point. If you are currently in a race with her, I advise you to stop running. The Universe is an Olympian sprinter, and this is a race you could never win. Trust me, I tried and lost. And I am a pretty good runner. Do yourself a favor and surrender. Let her guide your path.

FOUR

MY CATALYST FOR AWAKENING

"Recognize what is in your sight and that which is hidden from you will become plain to you."
—The Gospel of Thomas

Unbeknown to you, your life has hidden some of the very best gifts it has for you inside your most painful and challenging circumstances. If you are unaware of their purpose at the time they happen, such events may seem devastating to you. But I can assure you, it is in the dark, cloudy moments of your life that you'll learn the most about your power and natural abilities as a human being. Often it is from the painful experiences where we must stare directly into the face of our fears that we gain the wisdom and strength to become who we were meant to be and to do what we came to do. If we don't resist it, pain can teach us resilience and wake us up to our potential for greatness. It has been this way for our ancestors, stretching back through the millennia.

In *Discover the Power Within You*, Eric Butterworth recounts a Hindu legend of a time when all men and women were as powerful as gods and goddesses. Because the people had the tendency to abuse their power, Brahma, the leader of the Hindu pantheon, determined that the gods needed to take the power back and hide it where our kind could never find it again.

The council of gods discussed various places to hide humanity's power, but Brahma disagreed with every suggestion they made. If the powers were hidden deep in the earth's crust, he felt sure that one day we'd find a way to dig it out. If hidden in the deepest reaches of the ocean, he felt sure that we'd eventually learn to dive deeply enough to find it underwater. And if hidden on the highest of high mountain peaks, eventually we'd climb to the heights and find it.

Frustrated, the council gave up. "We don't know where to hide it," they said. "As you've wisely pointed out, there's no place on the earth or in the sea that humans won't eventually reach."

At last, Brahma had an idea. He told the council, "I know what to do. We will hide the power deep inside each person, for they will never think to look for it there."[1]

Well, the gods' decision apparently had a caveat, which was to allow *those who were ready* to find their power—for that is the way it happens. We humans are just tricky enough or clever enough that some of our kind—only a rare few for a long, long while—were able to find a way to circumvent the obstacle and veil that was put in their path. But today, the secret is out. Anyone who goes within can find their hidden power.

Of course, most of us don't stop to look within until we are forced to by life.

> Most of us don't stop to look within until we are forced to by life.

As I previously mentioned, as part of my numbing strategy for coping with discomfort, I began to date a man right after my divorce. He was Latin like me, with dark brown eyes, salt and pepper hair, and passionate. Since he lived in Florida, I started to commute to Miami on a biweekly basis, and although difficult at times, I was so excited that I ignored the fact that right from the start I was the only one doing all the bending, all the doing, all the traveling. At the beginning everything to me seemed amazing. I felt excited that I was with a man who was crazy about me. My boyfriend told me that I was his soulmate, that he had never loved anyone as much as me, and that we would be together forever. You get the idea. All that in a matter of a month? I guess it was sign number one to run!

After a year and a half, he was less complimentary. I no longer felt like I was his queen. I never felt like I was good enough, beautiful enough, or sexy enough for him. It was as if I had fallen from a high pedestal to the floor below, and my fall from the heights hurt. Different remarks he made about what I was eating, my appearance, and my choices affected my self-esteem. I was not getting the acceptance from my partner on a regular basis that I had hoped I would.

How did I put up with it, you may ask?

At the time I was unconscious of the reason, but now I know why. Simple: I too did not like myself, and consequently, it was not foreign to me to live with disapproval. What my boyfriend was saying sounded like the words I was saying to myself inside my head.

Since then, I've learned through various spiritual teachers that our intimate relationships act as mirrors to reflect to us our truest beliefs. What we perceive shows us all that needs to be examined, addressed, and healed. Every situation in our lives that reflects our behavior back to us is a chance to wake us up. I was just not trained to recognize it yet.

Every situation that reflects our behavior back to us is a chance to wake us up.

It is sad, but it is the truth when I say that I was not being kind to myself. Furthermore, since I did not like who I was, I was always chasing around trying to look like someone else. Much like a cell phone or computer operating system goes through periodic updates, I spent years "updating" my persona, becoming different versions of myself depending on whom I was with and whom I thought I needed to please. My biggest update, which also caused the most glitches when it was introduced, came when I let this man come into my life to define my worth.

More than once, we would fight, he would leave me, I would beg and plead for him to come back, and he would. Each time he came back, I received him with open arms. I was in a trance and complete denial as to how unfulfilling our relationship was for me. For him too, I am sure. I could see he was in pain, but I didn't want to let him go.

Soon I was living in a state of constant fear of abandonment, scared that he would leave me permanently.

To keep him happy, I began to gain weight and to dress and look more the way I thought he wanted me to look. Worse, I did so because I did not accept myself. I did not love myself. I had forgotten my worth. It was self-mutilation.

At the time I had little spiritual awareness, so I could not understand the true function of this man in manifesting my destiny. I later came to understand the reasons the Universe had put him in my path. Our unhappy relationship opened my eyes to my deepest wounds and beliefs. He was mirroring for me my lack of self-love, my fear of being alone, of not being good enough.

I had lost my self-love, self-respect to the point that I too began to believe that I was flawed. Now that I have the gift of hindsight I can see how the Universe was hard at work, using this man as an instrument to bring out to the surface all the issues that I needed to heal. As Gregg Braden says, "Intimate relationships are the ones who bring powerful mirrors that come to reflect to us the pieces of ourselves that we've lost, given away, or had been taken from us."[2]

When you talk about the perfect storm, I lived through it. This one relationship, singly, brought out not just a few things I needed to heal, but ALL my fears and childhood imprints and conditioning. Yes, it was the perfect storm.

In retrospect, I sometimes laugh at myself because I know now that I could have chosen to learn from joy. Instead I chose to suffer. Either way, happy or sad, the Universe teaches through experience. We stay on each lesson until we master it. But here's the thing, even when we think we've learned a certain lesson, the Universe may send a curveball to test us.

We stay on each lesson until we master it.

In my case, the Universe was hard at work, increasing the intensity of my lessons so I could awaken. At first, I didn't want to learn anything. I resisted the process. I didn't even want to acknowledge what I was supposed to learn. Then, I started to recognize that I was being taught and I began doing my best to participate. The purpose of this book is not to tell you all the different ways I felt used or hurt or betrayed. What matters is the incredible signs and circumstances the Universe used to shake me awake. If I stubbornly refused to learn a particular lesson, the more painful my circumstances became. I could not escape them. This was true in every aspect of my life, including in my relationship.

Despite my instincts telling me that I was more invested in the relationship than the man I loved, I chose to continue the relationship. It was easier for me to believe that my boyfriend loved me than to face the painful reality that he did not.

Everybody that loved me could see I was heading for a disaster, straight off the edge of a cliff. My nine-year-old daughter kept asking me, "How many more chances are you going to give him, Mommy?

When your children begin to draw your attention to the things you should see for yourself, it feels terrible. Not only was I losing their respect, I was setting the wrong example for my girls. They would be women soon, and I was teaching them that being unloved, and settling for an unfulfilling relationship was okay.

I looked in the mirror, and I could not even recognize who I had become. I had given away my power, my voice, my self-respect. *Where was the strong, willful woman I used to be? Is this the legacy I wanted to leave for my girls? Am I truly so unworthy that I must settle for so little out of life and from this man? What happened to me, God?* These were the burdensome questions that haunted me night and day.

Looking back, I think the reason I continued dating this man on and off for several years was that I did not have the energy available to look inward and find my power. I settled for temporary high of moments of pleasure when we were getting along. I became addicted to the relationship. It gave my brain a dose of dopamine.

I may also have been addicted to the pain the unhappiness was causing me. It is said that behind every addiction there is an emotional addiction. My emotional addiction was my fear of being alone. Breaking up and getting back together again may as well have been heroin in my veins, giving me the high and the lows and the illusion of feeling alive and dead all at the same time. The longer I stayed in it, the closer I came to my death.

I have fallen so low, I thought.

Then I discovered the one incredible benefit of falling low: The only way to go next is . . . up!

There is no surprise that feeling unhappy, empty, emotionally abused, unloved, and lost would eventually lead to a complete nervous breakdown. But it may surprise you that I look back now at this as a gift. It is how the Universe finally taught me a valuable lesson and propelled me onto a spiritual path where I could make an important journey of self-discovery.

The Universe will use any method necessary to communicate with us. We just need to be receptive to seeing and hearing the messages, something that for a long time I had refused to do. However, after many hard knocks, the Universe wore me down and I finally began to develop awareness. When I did, let me tell you, the signs were everywhere!

On a Sunday morning at the gym I put on my headset to listen to a podcast from one of my favorite teachers, the preacher Joel Osteen. It had been about two years since I listened to any of his sermons, but on an impulse that morning I reached out for his message. I clicked on the first sermon on the list, which was entitled "Step into the Unknown."[3] It was as if he was speaking directly to me.

The Universe was putting Osteen at my disposal to convey something of the highest importance. The message was so loud and so clear that I was shocked when I heard it. In my heart, I knew it was meant for me. He said that when we feel lost, we just need to ask God to show us our way home. As dark and confusing as the turns along the way may seem, we must have faith that God is our guide, much like a GPS in our cars.

Interesting, I thought. I had derailed from my path. Now I wanted to turn back, but I couldn't figure out how. The road seemed too dark and part of me had given up the hope of ever finding my way home to myself. I had forgotten one incredibly powerful thing: my ability to ask the Universe for help. I had forgotten what Osteen so opportunely reminded me of that morning. *I have a birthright to divine guidance, and all I need to do is activate it,* I said to myself.

The more I listened the more interested I became. I stopped my workout and sat down on the mat to listen. It was too important not to give it my full attention. Osteen said, "All too often we don't listen to the directions or signs the Universe sends us because we are too used to our regular GPS systems, which tell us exactly where we are going."[4]

Our car's GPS has a feature called a "route overview." If you click on that, it will give you all the details of your entire route. There may be 15 different instructions: "Travel 3 miles ahead, in 2 kilometers take exit 42, in 400 meters turn left at the next intersection," and so on.

You get the point, right?

Osteen said we are so accustomed to knowing the entire route ahead of time that we've become a bit complacent.

You are used to knowing where you are going, how long it is going to take, and what to expect. Not knowing where we are going makes us comfortable. We have become used to always knowing what steps are next even before we need to take them.

Similarly, God has a route overview of your life. Even before you were born, God has laid out your entire destination, and he is the one who knows the best way to get you there. The difference between God's route and our car's GPS route-overview is that God does not show us the entire overview. The Universe does not operate that way.

God does not tell you how it's going to happen, how long it's going to take, where the turns are going to happen and who you are going to meet. God guides you by only revealing one step at a time. You need to show God you trust him by taking that step into the unknown. When you do, God will reveal the next and the next step leading you to your destiny. The challenge is that we are used to getting the details.[5]

Yes, that's true, I found myself agreeing. Everything I was hearing made perfect sense. It is easy to step out into the unknown when we have all the answers, right? Well, guess what? The Universe was encouraging me to leap into the unknown without the overview. It was asking me to have faith without knowing anything and stop trying to control and supervise the process.

Osteen explained that if we chose to step into the unknown with God, doors we did not know existed would open for us. The right people would show up and the resources we needed would become available. He further said:

> *God is the headlight in your path. Much like your car's headlight. When you drive, the headlight illuminates only about 160 feet in front of you. Yet you do not stop driving because you cannot see the full road ahead. You keep driving, and as you advance, the headlights reveal the next 100 feet and so on. So why could you not do the same with God's headlight?*[6]

Astonished, baffled, and in complete shock, I kept listening. *It is not every day that God dedicates a podcast just to me,* I thought.

Osteen, aka the Universe, then said, "Step into the unknown because it's in the unknown where miracles await."[7]

I was being told not to be afraid to follow the Universe's signs, as they would lead me home. I had been lost for too long, and now I saw it was my chance to surrender to the Universe, so it could guide me. However, to do this, I would have to endure not knowing everything.

That morning I told the Universe, "Okay, you win. Show me the next step, and this time I will follow you no matter how unknown and dark the road may seem."

You won't believe what transpired next. The very same day, in the afternoon, the next step was revealed to me. While at yoga class with my boyfriend, I was sitting on my mat meditating when my heart began to pound quickly. I felt a terrible need to breathe. I was gasping for air and the room seemed so hot I thought I was going to pass out. I reached behind me for my water bottle and discovered that I had forgotten it in the car. I fought my thirst for a few minutes, but as time went by, the discomfort of my heart pounding became greater. I opted to run out of class, cross the street, and reach for my bottle in the car while taking in some fresh air.

As I reached for my bottle, the screen of my boyfriend's phone, which was in plain sight on the car seat, lit up in that precise moment from a message coming in. Coincidence or another nudge from the Universe? I read the messages, which ended up crushing the last unbroken part of my heart.

If my heart was pounding in the class before, you can imagine how much more intense it became from the shock. I rushed back to the class and tried to breathe through the pain. I felt as if my heart was going to burst out of my chest. I kept trying to keep up with the class, but I had the sensation that I was having a panic attack, and I could not tell a soul why. Just two weeks prior I had forgiven an indiscretion and here it was, another one. A new one. I felt my world was caving in.

When we arrived home, I went into my bathroom and fell to my knees on the floor. I cried so much. The pain was so intense that I just lay there for a while in the fetal position. I felt my interior come to pieces. It was a mixture of desperation, fear, pain, and betrayal combined. Not sure if it was my instinct speaking or that I had actually heard voices, I was told, *It's time. How much more can you take?*

At the same time, my fear also spoke: *What will your life be without him? You will be all alone.* Felt devastated. So many dreams, so many empty promises, and three and half years of giving, and now all I had to show for it was a bleeding heart and a broken fairy tale.

My inner voice spoke again. This time it echoed Osteen's sermon, saying: *The next step has been revealed to you. Are you going to step into the unknown? Are you going to trust God to guide you to your destination or are you going to stay lost on the road leading you to destruction?* It was so weird. It was as if a podcast was playing in my head and Osteen was still talking to me from earlier that day.

Although it may sound crazy to you, I did hear voices in my head. Also, I saw the image of my girls before me and I felt incredible love for them and a huge sense of protectiveness and responsibility for them. I grabbed on to the love that I felt for my girls and decided that they, as well as I, deserved more. That day with an exposed bleeding and broken heart, I ended the relationship.

Some of the most profound moments in life are those in which you find the courage to let go of what you can't change.

They say that some of the most profound moments in life are those in which you find the courage to let go of what you can't change. That night, I took the Universe's sign as my God-given direction and I stepped into the unknown. I surrendered my navigation to her in the faith that she knew best how to get me home. Perhaps the longest night of my life, it marked the end of a chapter and the opening of a new one for me and my children.

FIVE

THE BEST WORST THING THAT EVER HAPPENED TO ME

"The lower you fall, the higher you'll fly."
—Chuck Palahniuk

My breakup was like living in the middle of the tornado. Fully engulfed in grief, I cried for days on end without leaving my bed. More than losing the person I loved, I think what created the devastation was all the dreams, the plans, the life together, the illusions I had built in my head. That is exactly—it was the castle on a cloud that I had built in my head alone. None of it was real, especially for him. All these compounded by the fact that prior to this relationship, my life was already in complete unbalance and chaos was the perfect recipe to send anyone on off a cliff.

I almost feel guilty saying this again because anyone looking from the outside would have told you that I had a beautiful life of privilege and an amazing family. Yet, as I mentioned previously, I was extremely unhappy, I felt I had no purpose, I was unsure of my gifts, and worse, I had walked out of a marriage to a wonderful man. The rebound relationship I had used as a means to shield myself form having to deal with all the things I did not like about myself came floating to the surface. The pain of all these things combined sent me to a deep end and a nervous breakdown became imminent.

My panicky moments were scheduled. The days I had my girls, I put on a brave face for them. But the nights I was alone, I returned to my grief. I became used to being devastated. I was playing the Academy Award-winning role, my best, the victim. At one point I remember losing my voice because I had cried and screamed so much. "Why, why, why did you have to hurt me this way when all I did was love you?" I sobbed over and over. The constant screaming, crying, and pleading made my voice so hoarse that it finally conked out.

Consumed by heartache, I still couldn't understand why I had stayed so long in such an unhealthy and unfulfilling situation.

In retrospect, I had stayed because my desire to avoid the pain I was now in had been stronger than facing the truth that I was unhappy and that I had been betrayed by someone I really loved and trusted. That was why I had ignored the signs for so long that I needed to call it quits. I could not have allowed myself to acknowledge the problems in the relationship without acting on them, so I denied them.

I was scared to feel the absence of someone next to me. But instead of facing this, my biggest fear, I had chosen to take a daily dose of poison. At first, I was unaware of it. It came camouflaged by little lies. I chose to avoid the ultimate death—the empty pit in my stomach and the intoxicating pain that would leave me breathless and limp—and instead, settled for a daily and slow death by a thousand cuts.

You know what I am talking about, don't you? You have felt this also.

Well, that's how I postponed the inevitable.

I felt as if I had driven my car through a guardrail and my body was now smashed on the ground at the bottom of a cliff. Or as my younger daughter, Emma, said, "Your train has crashed into a tree."

The young are so wise. One night she told me, "God sends signs. And when you do not listen, God keeps sending you even bigger signs until he gives you a tree to crash into. That's what happened to you, Mommy."

Funny? Yes. But SO TRUE!

Emma is incredibly insightful and seems always to know what is happening in the depths of my soul.

My life came to a halt. The aftermath of the loss and betrayal was accompanied by all kinds of terrifying thoughts: *Now what do I do?*

What will happen to me?

Will I be alone forever?

What will I do with my time when my kids are not with me?

What if I never find another partner whom I love as much?

I felt uncertain and fearful. My entire life, beside the period that I was sent away to a boarding school from ages seven to ten, I had not been alone for a long time. I went from living with my parents to marrying Jeffrey, and even after our divorce, for a long period of time Jeffrey and I stayed under one roof co-parenting. After that, I went straight into my new relationship. So being alone was a foreign and scary concept for me. I was so scared of my life ahead. I wanted so much to see the overview of my route on the GPS, but there was no use. I understood I could only experience life one step at a time. The anguish was unbearable.

We must face a void when we decide to walk into the unknown and the space between the known and the unknown can be terrifyingly uncomfortable. It requires courage and patience to live in the void between what was and what will come to be, and patience had never been one of my virtues. One of my many lessons, and this is exactly what the Universe was asking of me.

Nights and early mornings were the worst. The mornings because, as I awoke, I would realize that my loss was not a dream. The man I had loved was gone, and I was alone. Panic would set in. As the day progressed, it was not as bad because I made myself busy doing anything and everything I could to distract myself and cast my fears into the wind of my activities.

Again, as night unveiled its dark skies, fear would come knocking on my bedroom door. It did not matter how much TV I watched or what I read to distract myself, the fearful thoughts in my head were so loud, so strong, so many. They had taken my soul hostage.

I cried.

I prayed.

I passed out.

I woke up.

As I wiped my tears, my ex-husband, Jeffrey, who had remained my friend and confidant after our divorce, wisely advised, "Find the gift in your pain."

I sat with this idea for awhile, confused. *How do I find a gift in pain?* I wondered. A gift was something I had always associated with pleasure. Pleasure was something absent of pain. Where was the gift? It seemed to me the Universe was asking too much of me—perhaps to get even with me for all the years that I had abandoned my spirituality?

What I did not know yet was that I was being tested, taught to find a seed of bliss in great grief. I was being directed to courageously pursue my destined path and offer my gifts to the world.

We all know stories of incredible pain and victory. People who come out of the darkness with a deep sense of gratitude despite horrific experiences. But when the hurting is happening to us, it's easy to lose perspective, wouldn't you agree?

I am neither the first, nor will I be the last, to experience betrayal, heartbreak, and loss. Pain, loss, and grief are universal human experiences. It is what we do with them that matters. Around this time, I read *Man's Search for Meaning* by Viktor E. Frankl, a remarkable book that I found so, so helpful. Pondering Frankl's words "If there is a meaning in life at all, then there must be a meaning in suffering. Suffering is an ineradicable part of life, even as fate and death,"[1] I asked myself, *What could the meaning of my suffering be?*

There is a dichotomy when it comes to the way we think about pain. We hate to feel it, and yet when it hits us we often make it a permanent part of our lives. Instead of letting the pain go, we attach to the suffering and stay stuck in our pain. Could it be that the pain in our lives makes us feel more alive than the joy?

Or perhaps pain attracts more sympathy than happiness?

Sadly, it is through our painful experiences that we learn the most about our inner strength. It is through our pain that we reveal to ourselves what we are made of at the core.

Then I asked a new series of questions. *What would have happened if I had not been so afraid of the pain of being alone, of starting over again?*

What if I had looked at pain through a different set of lenses, a different perspective?

Would I have stayed to stuffer for so long? Or would I have entered the storm and be done with it?

I am a firm believer that the Universe does not give us anything that we are not able to handle. She knows what our souls are made of and the extent of our true strength. The Universe knows what to put you through in order to get you closer to the destiny meant for you. The adversity and the hurtful circumstances we confront can bring out the best in us and make us more resilient and self-aware. As Marianne Williamson says: "Something very beautiful happens to people when their world has fallen apart: a humility, a nobility, a higher intelligence emerges at just the point when our knees hit the floor."[2]

Finding the Gift in My Pain

The way I saw it, I had two choices: I could let my painful circumstance rob me of my willpower and give up on life while I lay around feeling sorry for myself. Or I could fight to find some way to dig myself out of the mental and emotional hole that I was in. I decided to take responsibility for myself.

Of course, I had not willingly created the pain. I also did not deserve what was happening to me. But through the state of my energy I had somehow attracted this. That is the first fundamental truth of the Universe that I mentioned earlier, remember?

Looking back on it today, I am glad events happened as they did. Had they not, I would not be the empowered and grateful woman I am today, and you would not be reading this book and sharing my insights right now.

So how do we create and attract what manifests for each of us? This was a question I thought about for weeks and months on end and studied hard to answer. This is what I learned.

We are infinite, spiritual beings of light and our energy fields are made from powerful waves of vibrations that are influenced by our thoughts, experiences, and whatever is happening within us at any given moment. This is a crucial concept for you to understand if you wish to become more self-mastered. If you can grasp this, you will be able to turn any situation around by becoming more conscious of what you are cocreating in your life.

So far, I have not found a better explanation than the following one given by Gregg Braden. I hope it enlightens you as much as it did me.

Science has discovered a field of energy that is every-where, and we are part of it. It is a living, pulsing, vibrat-ing, throbbing field of energy. It is a real-life matrix, and this matrix is the container for the Universe itself and for all things that can happen in the Universe. It's the bridge between our inner and outer world. Everything that happens from within, our thoughts, feelings, emotions, and beliefs, is conveyed to the world beyond our bodies through this field. This field then acts as a mirror—a mirror in the world for what we claim to be true in our deepest, subconscious beliefs.[3]

Draw your attention to these key words: *our deepest subconscious beliefs.* The problem we have is that we are unaware of 95 percent of the thoughts we think. Yet this field responds to us nonetheless.

The good news is that we can also communicate with it deliberately. Do you see how important it is to become conscious of the energy we give our thoughts? We are constantly in creation-attraction mode—it is unavoidable.

You need to become fully aware about what you are cocreating with the Universe, just as I had needed to be more aware of what I was creating. Are you creating light or are you creating darkness? That is the question to ask yourself every day.

When our energy is low, so is our vibration, creating a field around us that leaves us unprotected and vulnerable to other people's low-vibrational energy. But when our energy is high, we vibrate at frequencies that are positive, such as the frequencies of peace, content, love, joy, gratitude, and safety, and attract the same. As Gabrielle Bernstein writes: "When you dwell in an energy of positivity and power, you become a magnet for miracles."[4]

We attract that which is in harmony with our current vibration.

The best worst experience that had ever happened to me was my breakup because it led me to take full responsibility for what I was attracting in my life. My emotional state had been extremely negative and low when my ex-boyfriend had come into my life. My vibration attracted him because he was vibrating on as low a level as me.

Even if the Universe had a better plan for me, unless I learned to change my vibration I was going to continue to attract similarly low-vibrating people.

Certainly, I could have chosen to ignore the new information I was learning about the Universe's law of attraction. I could have continued to stay bitter and depressed, blaming my ex-boyfriend for my circumstances, and why not? It's not like I did not have any reasons to complain and blame. I could have continued to play the victim.

Instead, I opted to take responsibility for what was happening to me and looked for the gift in my pain. I was willing to look inwardly, to change what needed to be changed, and to address what needed to be addressed to finally stop the cycle. Like the Buddha said: "Pain is an inevitable part of life. Suffering is optional."

One day, I closed my eyes and sat on the carpet in my bedroom crying, letting my tears wash away my pain as if they were detoxifying me. I heard an inner voice telling me that something needed to change, and I intuitively knew that I needed to reconnect with the spiritual person I once had been. This recognition gave me the strength to go deeper.

That day I saw that my outside was a mess, but my inside was worse. The way I had been living my life for the past ten years was no longer serving me. A major reboot of consciousness was needed.

When we are in pain, it is easy to forget what we have and focus only on what we lack. People can say "This will pass," "You will be fine again," "Forget about it and move on," "There are worse things in life, so get over it," and the list goes on. But getting out of this mindset can be difficult. Only we can arrive at the determination for ourselves of when we've had enough.

The minute you choose to look at your pain objectively, the meaning of the pain will shift. There is a freedom that comes from detachment. I am living testimony to this.

My liberation?

It came when I allowed myself finally to embrace the pain without the shame associated with my vulnerability. I stopped fighting the grief and invited it in. I allowed the pain that I was feeling to penetrate every part of my soul. Which was when I realized I was so much more powerful than my thoughts and my suffering I HAD THE POWER TO CHOOSE how I was going to react to life.

As Viktor Frankl writes: "Forces beyond your control can take away everything you possess except one thing, your freedom to choose how you will respond to the situation."[5]

It was not easy to get back on my feet, I will not lie to you. It required fortitude.

It took me almost an entire year of working, learning, and applying the lessons I was being shown. I had to work at it every day, several hours a day, taking a step forward and three back, and having the discipline and mental toughness to do it all over again each day. The tears were many and the fear was real.

It would have been easier for me to continue wallowing in my pain and staying a victim who questioned only the why of things. But I made the effort.

So, what was the first step, you may ask?

To make a decision to get better fueled by strong intention. That's how it's done. The instant you set an intention to change, you create a new vibration and a shift happens. It is as Wayne Dyer writes: "If you change the way you look at things, the things you look at change."[6]

I'd thought for a long time that I was weak, which was the reason why I had relinquished my power and forgotten who I was. When I chose to be brave, I changed my perspective. In accepting responsibility for my pain, I learned that I was strong.

I am more than just my thoughts, my body, and my circumstances. I am not defined by the "one who loves me" anymore or by what others think of me. I understand that I can overcome pain and not attach meaning to it other than the gifts it holds. I can endure, and I recognize that, in truth, all things pass. I know that a great power resides in me. I can choose how I am going to feel and what I think about my reality.

As the Buddha said: "What we think we become."

My Wings to Fly

Finding something that fuels your inner power is vital in helping you overcome adversity because this will be the thing that prevents you from giving up. For me, as I said, I held on to the love of my girls. Even when I was at rock bottom, I was never confused about my love for my daughters. I did not want my girls to know me as a victim or a quitter. I had always told my kids to be brave and never quit doing the things they believed in. I had always counseled them to do what was right, not easy, and to be grateful for life itself. If I did not take my own advice, how was I going to raise resilient women?

I began to lovingly and objectively look at myself. I stopped asking why things were happening to me and I began to ask myself empowering questions like: *If I knew I was going to die soon, what things would I like to be doing?*

Whom can I serve?

With whom do I want to share my life?

What do I want my legacy to be?

Whom do I love?

What I am most grateful for?"

Victor Frankl's line popped into my head: "He who has a why to live for can bear almost any how."[7]

I thought to myself, *My girls, Victoria and Emma, are my "WHY to live for" and they are definitely worth me surviving any HOW.*

My daughters are what I was most grateful for and it was my love for them that empowered me to transform my life. I wanted my girls to feel proud of who I was choosing to consciously become. I wanted to show them that the human spirit can conquer anything. They had witnessed their mother enduring a lack of love, disrespect, and mistreatment. Worse, they had seen my struggle, my grief, my self-judgment, and my unhappiness. Now it was time for my daughters to witness my self-love and courage and see me dig myself out of the hole that I created. It was my time to model resilience.

Finding something that fuels your inner power is vital in helping you overcome adversity

I have always felt it important not to hide my pain from my children. I want them to know what it is like to be human. This means allowing them to see me cry, hurt, reflect, love, and embrace pain.

While I was working my way through depression, I came clean with my girls about my inner doubts, pain, and dreams. I expressed my fears and my aspirations. I expressed my infinite gratitude for their presence in my life and for the strength I was able to derive from their love. I made sure that my beautiful daughters understood that the abuse I had allowed in my life was neither acceptable nor the norm in our society.

Most importantly, I wanted my girls to know that despite experiencing the dissolution of two significant relationships in my life I still believed in love.

Love is all there is. Just because it doesn't work sometimes, does not mean that it is not worth having.

I became an open book, completely exposed with both of my girls, especially with my older daughter. How could I ever expect my beautiful Victoria to trust her mother with her heartbreaks one day if I did not trust her with mine?

Intuitively, I knew that demonstrating how to mend my broken heart and transform my life would be empowering images for my girls to remember in the future. That desire ignited my soul with a burning intention fueled by love. My heart echoed the words of Lisa Nichols, who wisely said, "Our children are not looking at how we fail. They are looking at how we get up. It is not our perfection they are looking for. It's watching us stand up and shine in the face of such obvious imperfection."[8]

Once I formed my intention to model the best parts of humanity for my girls, I began to act in the spirit of the things that I wanted to see manifested in them. I began to embrace the things that I had in my life and started to show up each day expressing gratitude. I stopped blaming others and took full responsibility for my existence. Soon, a tiny ripple effect became a tidal surge. The more I showed up for life, the more life showed up for me.

The more I showed up for life, the more life showed up for me.

······································

SIX

A STRING OF MIRACULOUS EVENTS

*"Synchronicity: a string of events that happen in a way that
seems out of the ordinary. These moments of meaningful
coincidence happen when you are on the right soul path."*
—*Aletheia Luna*

It is said that when the student is ready, the teacher
appears. Once I was ready, it was like everything in
the Universe was aligning to deliver me the ultimate
series of lessons it had been waiting to teach me. A
perfect storm had brought to the surface of my consciousness all the issues I needed to heal. Conditions
were right. Then the Universe put things in motion. An
incredible course of events took place to get me to where
I am today: writing to you about the intricacies of miracles and the Universe's nudges that guided me further

down my soul's intended path. It feels to me as if I have been preparing for this journey for many lifetimes.

Was it a random coincidence or divine intervention? I'll let you be the judge. In my opinion, the Universe will use any resource available to make miracles. In my case, the first miracle in a string of miraculous events was that I reconnected with my old friend Debra Bash, who had been my personal trainer many years before. I had not seen her for 15 years. But for some reason I saw her name on Facebook and we chatted briefly. Then we met in person to catch up on both our lives. I was fresh out of my breakup, so I was really feeling lifeless. It had been almost a month and I had not gone out once with anyone. Yet, that day something in my intuition told me to get out of bed, put on some makeup, and get out of the house.

The Universe is always speaking to us, sending us little messages, sending the right people, causing coincidences and serendipities reminding us to stop, to look around, to believe.[1]
—Nancy Thayer

I was a bit worried about having Debra see me in my low state after so many years. I did not want to cause a bad impression, so I made a real effort to do my hair and makeup and look as decent as I could. We exchanged stories about our divorces, work, kids, life, and so forth—the things women who are old friends usually talk about. I cannot even remember how we got on the subject, but she mentioned that she thought I'd like the book *The Universe Has Your Back* by Gabrielle Bernstein.

Little did I know that this brief encounter, which lasted less than two hours, and Debra's casual mentioning of a book was going to change the direction of my life to such a degree. But it did. I have not seen Debra since that day. Strange, don't you think? Could it have been divine intervention, a message from the Universe being delivered by an old friend?

As soon as I got home, I downloaded the recommended book and began to read it. I could not put it down. Bernstein was advocating something that sounded crazy to my ears back then. Her advice reminded me so much of Mama Rosita's teachings when I was a child and of the message Joel Osteen preached. In essence, her message was: *Let go and let God.*

I was being guided to completely let go of my fear and control in the belief that the Universe would take care of me. I was asked to trust that everything that had happened and was currently happening for me was happening for my highest good.

I took this advice to heart. In the beginning, I struggled and repeatedly failed at letting go. Even when I thought that I was surrendering and trusting the Universe, I was still trying to keep some control for myself. It was unconscious. I did not even know that I was doing it. Control was so engrained in me that I was unaware that I was doing it.

I began to put what I was learning to the test. I relinquished control and looked for signs from the Universe. They are always there, remember? You just need to be mindful enough to see them. One of my signs is the number 13, a number that has followed me as far back as I can remember. Anything monumental in my life comes with the number 13 in it.

I was driving to Napa Valley from San Francisco and my GPS was sending me through all kinds of little roads and too much time had transpired with no real way for me to know if I was indeed going towards Napa. I began to get anxious. There had been many times before when my GPS sent me on a wild goose chase. In frustration I pleaded, "Please Universe, tell me that I am going in the right direction." I had not eaten all day and was exhausted. As I said this, I looked to my right and there it was, a big antique door by a gas station with the number 13 on it. That was my cue, and guess what, just as I turned the corner there was a big sign with an arrow saying "Napa." All I could say was amen.

Another example of asking the Universe for help and trusting her to guide you was when I was thinking of going to Peru, one of my favorite places in the world, to see a particular archeological site. I was doing research for a book and came across a site discovered in 1996 by José Luis Delgado Mamani between the town of Puno and Juliaca. It is a carved door in the mountains which is known as *la Puerta de Hayu Marca* or *Arámu Muros* (the Gate to the Gods). This door, or stargate, according to the locals, is a gateway to another dimension. Seeing it became an urgent goal for me. But since it is in a remote area in the mountains of Peru and I'd be going alone to see it, I was concerned for safety and logistics.

I was at the airport in Toronto on my way to Sedona, Arizona, to attend a conference on spirituality and as I sat on the plane I closed my eyes and began to dialogue with the Universe about la Puerta. "I would love to go and I will leave it to you to work it out and show me the way." I closed my eyes and rested on the five-hour flight.

You won't believe what transpired next. I got to the hotel with two hours to spare before the conference began. I enjoyed a massage in the spa and then eagerly reported for the opening session of the conference at 7 p.m. I was mesmerized by speaker after speaker, and then the last speaker of the evening came on stage and I nearly fell from my chair. The announcer tasked us to please welcome . . . Don José Luis Delgado Mamani. Yes, that's right. The man who discovered the door! What do you think about that?

Coincidence or divine guidance?

Through setting intentions and stepping back we allow miracles to take place.

After the presentation, I ran to Don Jose and introduced myself. Don Jose gracefully gave me all the information I needed, and if that was not enough, helped me plan my trip. He put me in touch with his people in Puno, who booked my hotel, and also recommended a trustworthy guide he uses for his own tours. I was set.

Two months later, I went to Peru and at 12,656 feet (3,830 meters) above sea level, I accomplished my dream to see and spend time viewing an incredible wonder.

I have recently understood that letting go of the control and the worry of how things will happen is not quitting or giving up on the beautiful notion that nothing is impossible if you believe wholeheartedly. I remain firm in my adherence to that belief. Rather, I have learned that it is powerful to take a step back and relinquish attachment to the outcome you want and then dialogue with the Universe about it. It is through setting our intentions and stepping back that we allow miracles to take place. In the giving of space, we allow the Universe to do her job.

SEVEN

....

BEING THANKFUL FOR THE CLOSED DOORS

"When you think you are surrendering,
surrender some more."
—Gabrielle Bernstein

E qually important to your willingness to let go is knowing *when* to let go. Sometimes, even after trying you're hardest and giving it your all, the Universe makes you wait for a specific outcome. When delays occur, it can be because the Universe plans to bring you a better gift or show you a higher path or a better possibility. As Joel Osteen says, "Be grateful for the closed doors."[1] I now understand the Universe will open doors, but she will also close doors not meant for us. It just means the Universe has a different plan.

I think that it is appropriate to give you an example of how this has happened for me since we are talking about the principle of being grateful for the closed doors. When I completed my undergraduate education in 1993, I wanted to be a lawyer more than anything in the world, since as far as I could remember there had always been a desire in me to help people. I wanted to become a lawyer not for prestige or money, but because I wanted to help those who could not defend themselves.

I come from a long line of doctors in my family, but I never developed the same love for the art of medicine as my forbearers, so I just couldn't pursue that destiny. Being a doctor is an amazing vocation because, what better gift is there than giving someone the gift of life? But it just wasn't for me. When I was very young, I became fascinated by the television lawyer Perry Mason. I said to myself, *If I can't give someone the gift of life, the next best thing is the gift of freedom!* That was my dream. I wanted to be like Perry Mason.

If you asked anybody that knew me back then, they would tell you that I busted my ass to get into law school. Unfortunately, due to English not being my native language, I was not able to score high enough on the LSATs to be accepted. I studied so much, and I honestly tried everything I could think of within the means

I had to raise my score, but my efforts were futile. My score was borderline.

To increase my future chances, I decided to pursue a master's degree in criminal justice, hoping this would give me a bit more weight on my law school application. I graduated from that program in 1995 with an impressive A-minus average, but those studies combined with my LSAT score still were not enough to get me admitted!

I lived and breathed the prospect of going to law school for several years. I had great letters of recommendations. I even submitted studies to the Admissions Department that showed that a lower LSAT was no indicator of the actual success a student would have. Nothing helped. Disappointed, I could not understand why I could not accomplish this objective.

The Universe understood more than me.

Today, looking retrospectively at my life choices, I know that law school would have limited what the Universe had in store for me. Had I been accepted to law school, I would not have had the opportunity to cofound Embanet. Embanet was an ed-tech company that helped working professionals improve their lives through continuing education, which we delivered online to them. In 1996, Jeffrey and I set the intention to touch the lives of over one million learners worldwide, and by 2006 we had done that and more. The dream that we began working toward from our bedroom grew to become one of the leading providers of distance education in the world. Therefore, I ended up having more impact on people's lives than I had ever dreamed I would as a lawyer. As Osteen says: "God can see what you can't see"[2]

The Universe understood more than me. My true desire was to help people. Law school was only a means to an end. After that door was closed in my face, the Universe gave me precisely what my heart desired through another avenue. It will do the same for you.

Ultimately, you need to trust that if something does not happen in the way you envisioned despite your efforts, it does not mean that your dream won't come to pass.

Because of founding our company, a single mother could go to school to improve herself and upgrade the life of her family while she also worked. We were making it possible for people who otherwise could have only aspired to become more than they were to change their lives and futures by making education available to them.

So, you see, I never abandoned my dream of helping people. The Universe just chose a different venue for me to throw my energy into.

There are many routes to get you to any destination. Ultimately, you need to trust that if something does not happen in the way you envisioned despite your efforts, it does not mean that your dream won't come to pass.

I took responsibility for my grief and I began to feel empowered.

My failure to get into law school is just one example of the many doors the Universe has closed for me to propel me closer to my ultimate destiny. Once I understood to surrender to the oversight of the Universe, I kept learning and I kept practicing gratitude. As I read and studied more about the art of surrendering, I began to apply the principles of letting the Universe guide my life. I took responsibility for my grief. I began to feel empowered. And I no longer felt sorry for myself.

Although I was still hurting very much from love dissolution, I started to have moments of peace and clarity that came from the acceptance and understanding that if the Universe closed the door to this relationship in spite of my efforts, it meant she had a better opportunity and life plan for me as had been the case with law school.

With this new mindset and acceptance, I could feel something shift inside me and I began to believe that things were not happening *to me*, they were happening *for me*.

EIGHT

GIVING TIME, TIME

"When we surrender our will to the power of the
Universe, we receive miracles."
—Gabrielle Bernstein

A lthough I was more open to listen to my intuition and trust the Universe, I still had many questions a year into my recovery from my breakdown. I had done a lot of work up to that point to overcome my grief and make peace with the real me, but at times I was still unsure of what I was supposed to do next. The voice in my head of my old self would every so often come to reclaim me, making me feel insecure and alone.

That's when another miracle happened.

At the risk of sounding crazy, I must tell you about the new voice that I heard. I had heard voices in the past, remember, but those voices felt like they were coming from inside my head, from inside of me, so I often shook them off. During the incident I am about to describe it was different.

The Universe *spoke* to me.

Yes, you read that correctly. I was driving back from Caledon, Ontario, after dropping my daughter Victoria for her equestrian training. The drive from Caledon to my home in Toronto is about 50 minutes long, and although long, it is a very pleasant drive because it takes me down narrow roads with green pastures on both sides.

That day it had rained. The sky was still looking dark and there was a smell in the air hinting of more rain to come. On the horizon, I could see occasional bursts of lightning. As I was looking at the beautiful scenery, I started to muse about how I was going to live the second part of my life. The usual fearful questions began to creep into my mind again, and that's when I heard—coming from behind me: "*Surrender the how.*"

My arms got goosebumps, and my first reaction was to turn around immediately to look at the back seat. For a moment, I thought I was going crazy. I was alone. The music was not on. It was just me and the voice that seemed to linger in my ears or my memory. Honestly, I do not know which it was, but I heard it again. The voice was firm, commanding, and clear.

Again, it said: *"Surrender the how."*

Because there was no question that I had heard it, I knew in that moment that I was being commanded to follow the Universe's instructions.

Surrender the "how."

I was not about to defy the Universe on this one. I was fearful of not following a metaphysical command. That voice was strong, and I did not perceive what it was saying as being negotiable. I had to do it. I knew that surrendering was not going to be an easy or natural thing for me to do; however, I began working on reprogramming my old, controlling habits.

From then on, I surrendered one day at a time. There were, for sure, many moments of peace and comfort in my days, times when I felt that I could sit through the discomfort of not knowing it all. But there were other moments of weakness. *How do I suddenly just let go of the way I have operated my whole life and trust the Universe?* I would wonder.

I have spent my entire life trying to control everything even though intuitively and intellectually I knew that none of us really controls anything. To know things intellectually is one thing, of course, but to act, integrate, and live in faith is a very different matter.

I began by simply challenging myself on a daily basis. I did not think of the future. I focused on surrendering for that day only. I played head games to get the upper hand on my brain's safety mechanisms, using affirmations like: "Fake it until you make it."

I told myself that surrendering was for a day only and for that day I just did not worry about the outcome of things. If something did not go my way, I did not attach energy to it.

I continued with my game, one day a time, until one day became a week, a week became a month, and a month became a year. In the process, I learned that if something does not happen right away, or as I would like, there's no reason to despair. I simply shift my thoughts from anxiety to hope.

Things happen according to the Universe's timeline not mine. And it's comforting not to have to run everything all the time! *It is comforting to know that I am not alone and that I do not have to carry the burden entirely by myself; I have an ally, a support, an advocate, a protector, a vindicator, and therefore I don't feel that I am alone anymore.*

These days, I choose to think that there is a reason for everything that happens. There is a lesson even in the things that I do not understand.

Months after I began my game, without even realizing it I had stopped living in anxiety and I was endowed with positivity. Instead of reacting negatively or fearfully to things, as I would have in the past, I would ask empowering questions when I hit a barrier. Here are three questions I highly recommend asking in such situations.

- What is the Universe trying to tell me?
- What is the lesson in this?
- What is the gift that I am being given here by not having this outcome realized?

By surrendering all my outcomes to the Universe, I learned that if things do not happen at all, it is because they are not for my highest and greatest good. If a door has closed, it isn't an appropriate door for me. If someone has come and gone, well, it just means a relationship was not meant to be.

I am now grateful for the door the Universe closed for me when that man betrayed my heart although I did not understand it at the time. I mistakenly felt that the Universe had let me down. Because I had tried so hard to save that relationship and make it work, I could not appreciate that the Universe loved me too much to let me stay in a life that was substandard to the one that she had planned for me.

God can see the bigger picture of your life. God knows where every road is leading. He knows the dead ends, he can see around the corner. For us it may look great, what we cannot see is that there is danger, heartache, trouble up ahead. A big part of faith is trusting God when you don't understand.[1]
—Joel Osteen

Remember all the road signs that the Universe sent to forewarn me? I had dismissed them because the road in front of me looked bright and clear. But then I got lost in the darkness.

The Universe can see things you cannot possibly see until it's too late. So, do not be deceived. Not everything that shines is gold, as the saying goes.

I used to think that surrendering was losing control. Now I know it is a type of faith, one that brings with it a higher probability that I'll get where I need to go. I choose to believe that the Universe is my friend and colluding with me to help me achieve my dreams. When you embrace this mindset, you're going to look for the lessons in everything that you encounter, good or bad, and it will help you see opportunities.

I began to understand that the Universe supports and protects me. As a result, I can look back at my pain from a distance now and see it as something which happened, so I could learn a valuable lesson. The lesson helped propel me at an accelerated pace toward my true destination.

NINE

....

MEDITATION

"Prayer is when we ask God for direction. Meditation is when we stand still and quiet long enough to hear the answer."
—Lisa Nichols

Remember how I told you about the three funda-mentals truths that I learned after my nervous breakdown and how the first and third were my most important discoveries? Truth one: Everything you experience, good or bad, is created by you. Truth three: You are not alone. Well, the minute I opened my heart and mind to new possibilities I began to experience all kinds of miracles in my life. And the more I began to reprogram my mind to focus on new thoughts and emo-tions, the more I began to tap into divine guidance.

As I changed into my empowered self, the Universe sent me an increasing amount of feedback through tiny miracles and serendipities. I started to communicate with the Universe regularly, asking her to guide me and reveal the next steps I should take in my life. I was walking through the unknown, so I had no map overview, no blueprint, no sense of clear direction for where my life was headed. Each day I prayed and meditated for guidance, for signs, for messages.

With meditation, I stumbled upon the key to the door that leads directly to the path of divine source. Many people try meditation and give up on it because they never feel able to quiet their minds. While I am not an expert meditation facilitator, here's how meditation works for me.

With meditation, I stumbled upon the key to the door that leads directly to the path of divine source.

I first heard of Transcendental Meditation through a podcast. It intrigued me that a lot of athletes and successful people use TM to enhance performance. I read their testimonials describing how it helps them to focus, reduce stress, retain memories, strengthen their immune systems, and improve their lives overall. I was sold. My first instructor emphasized the point that TM isn't a religion, but a lifestyle. I thought, *What do I have to lose in trying?*

This ancient meditation technique was brought to the West by Maharishi Mahesh Yogi in 1959 and it has become popular all around the world since then due to its simplicity. Right from the start, I really liked it because it did not demand too much of me as a beginner.

I started by meditating 20 minutes twice a day. My instructor gave me a mantra, a two-syllable word that I said in silence to myself, to keep me grounded and to train the monkey chatter. I did not have to say this mantra constantly. Unlike popular belief, I learned that successful meditation doesn't require us to quiet the thoughts in our heads! TM did not demand that I fight to focus or control anything. In fact, I was taught not to fight a single thought, but rather to welcome them and let them pass me through.

So, one piece of advice. Never ever try to train your mind to go blank. It's impossible. Within a few days of doing TM, I realized that having my mind blank and never having a single thought would imply I was dead. After that I was good with having thoughts and letting them pass through my mind without any resistance. What is interesting is that the more I practiced, the less

I resisted my thoughts, I just let whatever needed to surface come up.

When meditating these days, I always begin the session with a few deep breaths, after which I return to breathing rhythmically at a normal pace but still aware of my breathing. I close my eyes, lie down, or sit, taking the position I feel is most comfortable for me at the time, and then just practice going silent for 20 minutes. Surprisingly, the mantra takes care of itself.

When I first began, I noticed I had a lot of thoughts and I was aware of all the noises in the world around me, noises ranging from loud streetcars to the most minuscule sound of an insect. It was not easy at the beginning, as I felt very distracted, so much so, in fact, that yes, it would have been easy to give up as many others do. Sometimes I procrastinated before starting. And when I would put my timer on for the 20 minutes, each minute felt eternal.

But I persisted. Each day I made a point to tell myself, "It's just 20 minutes, Waleuska. In the scheme of a day, this time is nothing! And if it works, imagine the benefits that you can draw from this." Gradually my mind became less frenzied and meditation seemed easier.

I remember sitting in meditation one afternoon after about two months of practicing TM, and for the first having a few minutes of no active thought, just peace and silence. It was blissful.

As my mind began to go inward and reached deeper levels of my subconscious, the sounds outside me became less important, less noticeable. I was engulfed in such peace when I meditated that instead of dreading meditation, I began to look forward to my next session. The more I meditated, the more peace I would experience.

Gradually I became so in sync with my inner state that my body just knew when meditation would be beneficial. It was incredible. I began to mediate anywhere I could. At the airport while waiting for a flight. At the stables while waiting for my daughter. At home, in the car, at parks lying on the grass in connection with nature.

And then I started to have all kinds of visions and dreams and experienced being transported to different dimensions.

Through my meditation studies I learned that it is highly beneficial to spend the last three to five minutes of your day, just before you fall asleep, in gratitude, envisioning the things you would like to attract into your life. Why, you may ask? Because just before we are asleep is the time when the window to the subconscious mind opens. I believe it is the time when the Universe communicates most strongly with us through the sub-conscious mind and gives instructions and direction to the conscious mind. The key is to learn to be receptive.

Perhaps it will be appropriate here to share with you one of the many visions I have been given. Just before bed I meditated, as I usually do. I thanked the Universe in advance for her direction and guidance at a time when I was feeling so much uncertainty. The Universe knew I was feeling scared of standing in the void of the unknown. Then I closed my eyes and fell asleep.

That night she sent me a vision.

In a dream, in a vision of the night,
When deep sleep falls upon men,
While slumbering on their beds,
Then He opens the ears of men,
And seals their instructions.[1]
—Job 33: 15–16

I remember starting the dream in the middle of the ocean. I was right on the water, with my clothes on, as if I had fallen from a ship or something, but the dream did not tell me how I got to the middle of the ocean. I was scared. I could see no land near by and told myself, *I am going to die, I can't swim that far.* I saw the sky turning darker it was getting late and I was just there in the middle not moving. I could feel the fear and the coldness of the water inside me. Suddenly, I saw a shark at a distance. I panic when I saw it. Death was imminent.

I just knew there was no way out. I was going to die. I just felt that intuitively in the dream, "I am going to die," I said out loud.

As I saw the shark head toward me, in that moment, just when death was sure to come, I surrendered. I stopped thinking of ways to escape. I stopped trying to out swim the shark. I put my back on the water to float and directed my gaze to the sky, to the Universe, and I no longer fought my fate. I knew there was no point. The end of my life was at hand and I could not avoid it.

Suddenly, the instant I surrendered the fear, I began to experience the most incredible peace, love, and bliss. It is hard to describe what I felt. But it was a sense of heaven, of oneness. I no longer felt fear. I did not feel negative emotions. I was imbued only with love and acceptance.

The shark swam right to me, and at the point of contact, he fully submerged under my back. Carrying me on his back, he began to float me out of the ocean onto the shore. I could feel one with the shark as if I was the shark and the shark was me and I had a deep love for it. I was taken to safety and then I woke up.

The Universe was communicating to my subconscious, answering my prayer for guidance. She was showing me that the one thing I feared saved my life. I was being instructed to keep surrendering to my strongest fears and it became clear to me that the Universe was telling me that in my fear I was going to find my salvation and my strength.

The instant I surrendered the fear, I began to experience the most incredible peace, love, and bliss.

At first, I thought I was going crazy. I was afraid to tell anyone what I was experiencing, or worse, what I was seeing. I was afraid that if I told anyone, some authority would send me to the loony bin. I started to write down my experiences. Although I was not sure of the meaning of many of my visions, I felt confident that they were given to me for a purpose that eventually would be revealed to me.

The more I meditated, the more receptive I became, and the Universe began to communicate with me in an even stronger voice. She communicated with me through everything: people, books, podcasts, events, dreams, and circumstances. Nothing was random or co-incidental anymore. All sorts of events that at one point I would have dismissed as farfetched, began to feel intentional, and I felt fully engulfed in the gratitude of it all.

All sorts of events that at one point I would have dismissed as farfetched, began to feel intentional, and I felt fully engulfed in the gratitude of it all.

TEN

....

A NEW WORLD OF DISCOVERIES

"The only thing standing between your
future and you is you."
—Joe Dispenza

During my awakening, I started reading many books that inspired my soul. Through these books, I discovered incredible teachers. It was as if a divine force was aligning me with them. Before then, I'd had no idea who any of these teachers were nor that I was even going to be inspired to find my soul's purpose through their teachings. But that changed.

The Universe sure works in mysterious ways. Every so often on Facebook I would see an advertisement from the Gaia company. I kept seeing different buttons throughout the day, always offering me a different article. At first, I paid no attention to these ads. But as the days and weeks passed, Gaia kept popping up and since the Universe saw she was not getting my attention she used something she knows I love to get me to listen to her. As I mentioned before, I am fascinated by anything that deals with mysteries of the unknown. One night, the Gaia advertisement offered something entitled *Beyond Belief: A Glimpse of the Other Side.*

The Universe knew this title would catch my attention.

When I clicked on the ad, I saw I had landed on a pay wall, so I just closed the web page. You know what they say: Out of sight, out of mind.

A few days after, I was listening to a podcast and one of the paid advertisements was again this thing called Gaia. *Again,* I thought?

A few days later another title popped up: *Encounters with the Unexplained: What's Behind the Door in the Pyramids.*

Are you kidding me, I thought? Anyone that knows me knows my fascination with ancient Egypt. Since I was a little girl, I have devoured books on ancient civilizations and mysteries behind the creation of the pyramids. I was there in 1995, lucky enough to enter the royal chambers of the Pyramid of Cheops, aka the Great Pyramid of Giza due to its proximity to Giza's plateau. Nowadays, you are no longer able to do so.

At last this Gaia thing was starting to get my attention. I was seeing it so often and hearing about it from other sources that I began to think there was a reason for it. By this point, I was a lot more aware of the divine guidance of the Universe. I signed up and was not disappointed. This has been one of the best investments of my life because of what I have learned from the TV programs I've been able to watch. There is no doubt in my heart and mind that the Universe guided me to these offerings in preparation for meeting my destiny. As they say: There are no accidents in life, just messages.

The message from the Universe was clear. It was in this digital database of educational treasures that I was introduced to the concepts, principles, spiritual teachers, authors, and books that would teach and prepare me to obtain the knowledge, strategies, and tools I would need to manifest my intended destiny. The Universe was guiding me through coincidences to learn what I have learned for a purpose: to transcend to my rightful path.

Each of the books the Universe presented to me had a specific principle to reveal. Each introduced me to a teacher whose philosophy now guides my life and my actions, and to people like me, who emerged from the darkness into the light and dared to be vulnerable enough to put their walls down and expose their ideas nakedly, authentically, with the world.

I did not know as much as the teachers did, so I decided to study their words. I wanted to learn everything they knew. Every day I would read for hours on end, book after book, and I watched every podcast I could find. I listened to interviews they had given, I took their online courses, if they offered any, and made detailed notes on all I was learning and all I was immediately applying in my life.

Because of my studies, I began to change inwardly. I felt different and I began to envision all kinds of possibilities for my life. I was creating new neural networks and suddenly I was not stuck living in my past anymore but began to envision a future of unlimited possibilities. My brain, my thoughts, my emotions, and my behavior were changing.

Fear and death stopped knocking on my door at night.

Fear and death stopped knocking on my door at night. I felt empowered by the amazing things that I was learning from teachers such as Joel Osteen, Sabrina Heartsong, Marianne Williamson, Gabrielle Bernstein, Wayne Dyer, Brené Brown, Carlos Castaneda, Caroline

Myss, Neale Donald Walsch, Louise Hay, Gary Zukav, Lisa Nichols, Jean Houston, Michael Beckwith, Bradley Nelson, Robert Holden, Joe Dispenza, Gregg Braden, and Bruce Lipton, to name a few. These teachers have made it their lives' missions to share their truth and inspire people like me to change. Their words ignited a powerful desire in me to be of service to the world like them.

This was what was missing from my life. I had always known that I needed my existence to be for something meaningful, something that would be bigger than me. But now I wondered, *How can my life, my painful experiences and my discoveries, help others?* That was the question that consumed me and the one that I posed to the Universe the most often.

I put out my intention to become a teacher, a self-empowerment advocate, and I waited for the signs. I rose from one of my meditations, weeks later, with the burning desire in my heart to write a book. It was an instant "knowing." A seed of desire was planted in me. The writing was going to be my way to be of service to readers like you. It resonated with my heart: In that moment, I had no idea yet what the actual details would be. I just knew that I had to transform my pain into a gift.

Since childhood I've displayed an aptitude for writing, and when I began to write, it was the best decision that I made. I started to exercise my writing muscle with a monthly blog. I wrote each month about my life, my experiences, and the transformation that I was seeing in the world. This inundated my soul with fresh air. I found blogging therapeutic and my entire being uplifted. Writing gave my life new purpose and meaning. I found myself suddenly motivated by new dreams, new goals, new intentions, and gratitude.

Each morning I would awaken with excitement in anticipation of all the amazing things that I would learn that day. And I found renewed strength inside me, like I had activated a dormant power. It is true what people say: You don't know how strong you are until you have no choice but to be.

I took action. I made a phone call to a spiritual teacher named Sabrina Heartsong, in California, and asked her to help me clarify my objectives and move forward with my intentions.

ELEVEN

OVERCOMING EARLY CHILDHOOD CONDITIONING

"Whatever we plant in our subconscious mind and nourish with repetition and emotion will one day become a reality."
—*Earl Nightingale*

I f you've never previously done any work to become aware of your patterns and childhood conditioning, consider starting out on your path to heal your life with this. Your childhood conditioning is at the core of all your issues as an adult because they are the root from which you birthed all your beliefs and perceptions. There are a lot of resources designed to help people be successful in this endeavor.

My intention here is not persuade you to take a particular course of action. My sole purpose is to describe for you the systems that have worked for me. Ultimately the decision whether to try something or not is entirely up to you. With Sabrina's assistance, I began to do a lot of inward work taking me back to the very beginning of my childhood and decoding the negative patterns and limiting beliefs that I had formed between the ages of zero and ten.

According to biologist Bruce Lipton, only 5–10 percent of our awareness comes from the conscious mind. The conscious mind is the one responsible for our short-term memory and analytical thinking. The other 95 percent of everything we think, feel, and believe, including our habits, relationship patterns, and long-term memory, all reside in the subconscious mind along with all its programming.[1] Guess where all that 95 percent is rooted from? Your childhood conditioning. Astonishing!

Think of the human brain as a computer. According to Lipton: "From the age of zero to ten your brain is in a programmable stage. A child is in a state of hypnosis, everything it observes, it downloads as a program."[2] It is in this stage that our brains are conditioned and encoded with positive as well as negative perceptions about the world learned from our primary caregivers.

Emotional freedom technique expert Robert G. Smith explains: "Your subconscious mind begins to record all these experiences as beliefs, stores them and makes them real to your subconscious mind later in life."[3]

Everything that we learn at an early age forms our personal belief system and emotional patterns; and as adults we judge the world based on those same belief patterns. These patterns are engrained in our subconscious minds and influence every part of our lives: our relationships, our vocational choices, our fears, and our health. "The brain becomes a set of automatic programs that become 95 percent of who you are by the age of 35. We have a set of memorized behaviors, perceptions, attitudes that function just like a computer program."[4]

According to chiropractor Bradley Nelson, "Unlike the conscious mind that forgets things like where you left your keys or what you had for breakfast, the subconscious mind is a holographic archiving computer recording every moment of our existence."[5] Our subconscious minds become the lenses through which we view and judge ourselves and others.

Theta healer Esther Kochte says that if as a child you heard your primary caregiver tell you things like "You are difficult, you were a bad boy, you don't deserve that, you are not good enough, you are not smart, you are dumb," then these ideas will hold an emotional charge with a strong stimulus stored in your brain.[6] You store them and it makes no difference that you heard them at age four instead of age 40. You can be 40 years old and these conditioned beliefs will show up in your adult life and manifest in all kinds of unwanted ways.

Our subconscious mind does not recognize time and space. Whether something was said 30 years ago or yesterday, it is all the same to the subconscious mind. You form beliefs based on what you repeatedly heard your caregivers tell you or how you observed them deal with their world.

Fortunately, we can change these codes by learning to identify and heal the beliefs.

I don't know about you, but I had four primary caregivers: my mom, my nanny, my dad, and my grandma. Those four people were responsible primarily for all my early childhood conditioning. The first step that I had to do to overcome my early childhood conditioning was to identify all the negative and positive characteristics of each of my caregivers. I identified how those negative characteristics made me feel *as a child*, not as an adult, and what the things were that I needed most from these individuals as a child.

It was an eye opener for me to discover my childhood patterns. I will share them with you here to give you an idea of what you might find when you look at your own belief system.

It was an eye opener to discover my childhood patterns.

As a child, I felt that I was not loved enough by one of my caregivers. I felt I was not good enough. I often felt that I was all alone and fearful of being abandoned by at least three of my caregivers. This is very sad for me because, as a child, the most important things for me were to feel loved and accepted, protected, and secure.

Now, are you ready for the shocking part? According to Gregg Braden: "We often attract people, situations, and opportunities that demonstrate the negative characteristics that we liked least from our caregivers. We attract them because we have placed an emotional charge on those characteristics and that charge becomes the magnet."[7] Upon closer examination of my beliefs, I was surprised that this, in fact, was the case for me.

I can tell you that during my perfect-storm relationship, my boyfriend had displayed all the characteristics I disliked most in my caregivers. I apparently unconsciously attracted negative things reminiscent of my childhood into my life because those were the characteristics familiar to my subconscious. My ex-boyfriend was emotionally unavailable, detached, critical, and someone who betrayed my trust. Consequently, he triggered all my patterns. I was criticized and betrayed, so my fear of not being loved enough came to the surface. I felt that I was not loved, so my fear of not being good enough also surfaced. Since my ex-boyfriend was not emotionally available to me, my fear of abandonment exploded at the cellular level, making me live my life in constant stress, anger, and fear. That was a great recipe triggering my body to become ill.

The things we want to give most are the very things that we needed most as a child.

My spiritual teacher Sabrina Heartsong explained to me that the things we want to give most are the very things that we needed most as a child. No wonder I went out of my way to please my ex-boyfriend, to love him, to protect him, to take care of him. Now everything made sense. My unmet needs as a child had manifested into my ex-boyfriend. Without realizing it, I wanted to give him all that I had needed as child.

And what about you?

What were your unmet childhood needs?

What do you most want to give?

Look at those two questions and the answers will give you clues to your patterns.

We are resourceful beings. According to Braden: "We become resourceful at finding other means to either meet our needs or protect ourselves from the pain of not having those needs met. For example, if it is attention that you are lacking, some children will begin to act up, get into trouble to get attention. If it is acknowledgment that they are lacking, some kids will go into sports to get their validation that way."[8]

We also then need to look at adolescence and adulthood. How did my childhood conditioning show up for me in adolescence and adulthood? I began to excel academically to please my dad and to gain the love of my maternal grandfather. I knew they both valued the intellect, so I figured that if I excelled they would love me. As an adult, this manifested into a constant striving for perfection.

Here's another example. In childhood, I felt emotionally disconnected from my mother due to her being unavailable, so what did I do? I made a strong maternal connection to my grandmother and my nanny instead of her. That was my creative way of meeting my need for maternal love and connection.

As a child, my family had moved often, to different cities in different parts of Nicaragua—and then to Canada. I never felt connected. As an adult, my negative emotional charge for this manifested in a resistance to change.

As a child, so that I could attend the best schools I was sent away to a boarding school in a different city than the one where my family lived. As an adult, of course I know this was done for my benefit. But as a child of eight, it felt like abandonment. I remember hiding under my bed so that my parents would not be able to take me and leave me at the school.

An emotion I felt as a child that was intensely painful was that I always felt alone. How did this pattern of loneliness manifest in my adult life? It manifested in a strong need for companionship. I was frequently fearful of being alone. This fear had drawn me into relationships that were damaging for me; I stayed in an unhappy and unfulfilling relationship because I did not want ever to feel lonely.

Now, I understand that it was because I did not want to relive the emotions of my childhood that I made those choices. However, prior to doing the work of overcoming my childhood patterns, I was completely unaware of the roots of my behavior.

Another example of how my imprinting shows up is in me not completely letting go and fearing being fully loving or fully belonging to someone. As a child, I perceived myself as being abandoned by the people I loved. My nanny, Maria Isabel, was in many ways my mother for a long time because my real mom was very busy working. Unfortunately, Maria Isabel was young and unstable. Each time she and my mom would get into an argument, Maria Isabel would retaliate by leaving. She would take off for weeks at a time. I would go into such withdrawal from her absence that my parents would go find her and beg her to come back.

Doesn't that sound like someone in my later life?

My father was my idol as a little girl. I guess I am not unique, as I see that all the time. Little girls just love their dads. When I was little, he left the country for some time and I would not eat. I became sick from missing him, at which point he had to return. Also putting a charge on men coming and going.

My point is that as children we can't use logic or discern the real reasons why adults sometimes do what they do. In my child's unfiltered mind, what I perceived was that the people I loved most and relied upon were leaving me.

My subconscious mind learned to associate needing and loving someone with the painful possibility that they were going to leave me. This was in my young perception a very real possibility. So, not completely giving myself to someone I loved, or not allowing myself to fall entirely in love, was my way of protecting myself from the disappointment. The sad part is that it never worked. I got hurt just the same.

This imprint played a huge part in both my marriage and the relationship I had after my divorce.

This is how your early childhood imprints will show up throughout your lifespan.

Sabrina explained that I had to go deeper to address and heal my wounds and learn to release the emotional charge on each of the imprints above. She was clear that if I did not, I would continue to attract the same hurtful relationships I had in the past because the purpose of the patterns was to bring to the surface the things that I insisted on hiding from myself.

Over a period of a few years, I learned to fulfill my unmet needs myself, internally. If it was love I was needing, I gave it to myself. If I felt alone, I told my inner child that she was never alone because I was with her—something that still is challenging for me. If I felt I was not good enough, I immediately shifted to a mode of giving myself appreciation for the qualities that I have. If I felt the fear of being abandoned, I turned to gratitude for my children, for my friends, my family, my mother who is always here with me. I began to see that the fear was only in my mind and that, in truth, I am never alone. I am always surrounded by those I love.

After much work on childhood regression, it all finally began to click for me. I now knew why I did the things that I did, where they rooted from, why I resisted certain things, and the reasons why I was attracting the same kind of people and painful experiences into my life. As Sabrina pointed out to me, "The relationships we have with others are a direct reflection of the relationship we have with ourselves." It was now clear to me that all these years, I had been hiding my wounds and grasping for my childhood unmet needs to be met in my adult relationships.

I discovered how unconscious I was to my limiting beliefs. Even if I wanted to change, the part of me that was conscious was fighting against the 95 percent of me that was unconscious. I had to do a symbolic brain surgery, open the brain and rewire the hardwire programs of my childhood and adolescent years.

When I began to understand the reasons why I did what I did, the way to change them became easier to discern and achieve. I finally could connect to a more hopeful future. To me, it was like finally lifting a veil or removing cataracts from my eyes that had clouded my ability to see clearly, and I began to experience my true power. I began to invest fully in myself. I began to nurture myself and to align my life with my soul's purpose.

> When I began to understand the reasons why I did what I did, the way to change them became easier to discern and achieve.

How can you know what your soul purpose is? A soul purpose is a desire that takes seed inside of you and resonates in every fiber of your being. It is a desire that comes from your highest and purest intention to serve. And although it is not self-serving, it is rewarding. It is something that you desire to do with unmeasurable passion. As Sabrina says, "A true desire is a soul's whisper. It is the way our souls communicate with us."[9]

My desire to write about my experiences grew until I felt a burning flame inside of me to write this book for you. Even as I began to write it, I kept asking in my head, *How do I write this? How do I structure it? How do I write in a way that will inspire? How do I even get it published?* The more questions I asked, the more anxiety began to take control of my being.

It takes constant work to remain in a state of spiritual equilibrium. It is not easy. If it were easy, then everyone would be making the changes they needed to make readily. From chiropractor Joe Dispenza I learned that whenever your brain senses you are changing, your body will crave to reassert your old self. It is easier for your brain to bring you back to the familiar and that is why it is not easy to change.

The body wants to take you back to the way you were, to always thinking about your present and future based on the same painful and fearful experiences of the past. That is what your brain is designed to do. It is designed to keep you safe. As Dispenza says: "The brain will always bring you back to the old thoughts so that you can make the same choices, to lead you back to the same actions and behaviors that result in the same old familiar experiences and the same limiting beliefs and emotions."[10]

While writing, I could feel my body pulling me back with fearful thoughts like: *What if I cannot write it? What if I am not talented enough? What if I fail? What if nobody likes it? What if nobody buys it?* It began to trigger my "I'm not good enough" childhood pattern, but at least I was conscious of it and know what steps to take to address it.

The way to change a pattern is by reprogramming the brain. As Dispenza explains: "True transformation comes when we break free from the chain of emotional addictions, when we begin to go in the operating system where those programs exist and we begin to make transformational changes."[11]

Just because I was having a thought didn't mean it was true.

Luckily for me, by this point, I was awake and aware of my thoughts, behaviors, and the power that emotions have in my life. When I would notice that I was doing the very thing that I was supposed to surrender, I would immediately shift my thoughts and my feelings. I could hear the chatter in my head telling me, *Yes, Waleuska, you are right. You are not a good writer and you have no experience with publishing books.* So, it became a war at the beginning for me. The best weapon for quieting and weakening the monkey mind was in not attaching energy to my leaping thoughts. Just because I was having a thought didn't mean it was true.

When I would tell my spiritual teacher, Sabrina, that I was feeling pulled into the sea of doubt, she would say to me, "Leave it to the Universe to figure out the how. The how is not up to you." I loved her for always reminding me of this: the same phrase I had heard the Universe tell me in my car, remember? "Surrender the how." This phrase is now engraved in my subconscious and I make good use of it each time my body feels uncomfortable with my physiological changes. Each time I experience anxiety, her phrase serves as an anchor, bringing me back into alignment with empowering thoughts.

I now know to set my intentions, feel them, thank the Universe for them, and let go of any attachment to the outcome. It is then up to the Universe. If you are wondering, these are the four steps of manifestation.

1. Intend
2. Feel
3. Thank
4. Let go

You see, transformation is not the absence of doubt and fear. Not at all. It is having awareness and a strong "bounce-back muscle" and faith to repeatedly center yourself. You allow your fearful emotions to go through you, you observe them, you face them, but you do not attach energy to them. If you learn to do this, it is a sign you are evolving.

As Marianne Williamson says, "The path to spirituality is one in which when we fall into the valley of darkness, we have learned how to get ourselves out it. It is not about suppressing our emotions, rather about bringing them up so we can place them on a path to true healing."[12]

Even as I write this book for you, the Universe had not yet shown me *how* the book will get to you. I am simply letting the Universe guide my words, which pour straight from my heart on to the page. I am sitting in the unknown, having nothing but a burning desire and intention. I trust that the Universe will continue to reveal to me the steps I need to take. I trust that the Universe will manifest the right circumstances, the right opportunities, and bring the right people so that my dream of helping you learn from my life experiences puts this book in your hands.

> I trust that the Universe will manifest the right circumstances, the right opportunities, and the right people.

TWELVE

TAPPING INTO YOUR
DIVINE ESSENCE

"I'm realistic. I expect miracles."
—Wayne Dyer

I worked diligently for months with Sabrina, and our focus evolved from working on healing my inner child to working on the amazing power of manifestation. I had always looked at affirmations as a type of prayer and prayer as key to the manifestation of my dreams and desires, but I now understand that I had been missing crucial pieces of information.

The words we use in affirmations and prayers carry power. I learned that the Universe does not know tenses. It only knows the present moment. Hence, when you speak to your divine source, you need to speak only in the present tense and as if you are already enjoying the things that you want to manifest.

The Universe interprets affirmations such as "I want more money" or "I want a loving partner" simply as "want." Wanting implies you do not have it and so this kind of affirmation tells the Universe that you are in a state of lack so you will be wanting forever.

The Universe will only ever mirror back to us the states we project. As Wayne Dyer writes, "You do not attract what you want, you attract what you are."[1]

When you affirm to the Universe "I am abundant" and "I am manifesting a loving partner" the Universe registers this as something already manifested and echoes back into your life more of the things that you are affirming you already have, which in turn brings you what you in fact want.

Furthermore, the Universe does not understand the negative tense. When you say, "I don't want to get hurt," the Universe hears, "I want to get hurt."

When you say, "I don't want to be poor," the Universe hears, "I want to be poor." We spend too much energy thinking in the things we don't want and less on the actual thoughts we do desire. Instead, focus your thoughts on the things you like to manifest as already manifested.

Do you see now why so many times we attract the one thing we say we don't want?

This discovery was incredible! The more I read about manifestation and attraction, the more I noticed that all the teachers were saying basically the same things. Perhaps they used different methods, but the underplaying message was the same.

The Power of I AM

There is a huge power in the phrase *I AM*, a power that comes from God. It is the name God told Moses when they first spoke: "I AM that I AM."[2] So when we say "I am . . ." we invoke the power of God in us.

With practice, I learned to be careful of the words I place next to my I AMs because whatever follows your I AMs you ignite with power. We are the expression of God, so we have God in us. As a child, Mama Rosita had told me I was created by God as you probably have been told by your parents. However, nobody had told me that since I was created by God, I too am God! "God created you, and therefore, you possess all the qualities of God, just as you possess the genetic information of your earthly parents and ancestors."[3]

I now say and feel my affirmations. "I am love, I am prosperous, I am worthy, I am healthy, I am happy,

I am grateful, I am enough, I am strong, I am in love, I am a renowned author."

When you speak your I AMs, invoke and connect to your godly power by claiming those things from the quantum field of possibilities as your birthright. State that you *are* whatever you desire, as James Twyman says: "You are claiming that you are one with the desired state of the object."[4]

Wayne Dyer similarly asserts: "Your awareness that God isn't something external to you, but rather a portion of yourself is truly a giant step in your spiritual evolution."[5]

Incredible, don't you think? It feels amazing for me to wake up and claim my true nature by speaking the words "I am God," I am the Universe, I am the earth." It's true, we are! We are one with the Divine.

Twyman describes the mirroring force of God with these words: "When you say, 'I AM THAT' to God, God doesn't answer you saying, 'You are.' The Creator replies 'I AM.' In other words, God is saying, 'You claim it, then I claim it too, for we are one.'"[6]

This is just beautiful!

Manifestation Is Fueled by Emotion

Now that you have learned that your affirmations must be made in the present tense as if you already had them, you also need to learn to feel them in your body. Saying them is not enough. To manifest that which you desire, you need to speak the language of your body and the language of your body is your emotions.

Without firing an emotion in the brain that's associated with the sensations of already having that which you are affirming, an affirmation remains empty words. Manifestation expert, Joe Dispenza says: "Affirmations don't work because a person can say all they want 'I am healthy, I am abundant, I am free,' but that thought never makes it past the brain stem to reach the body."[7] It is only in the feeling of such intense emotion that you connect to your body and that is when you now have the power to manifest.

Once I had a grasp on what empowers affirmations, I made a recording of the things I wanted to experience in my life, and those became my affirmations throughout the day. Each time I said them, I connected my body to the emotion of having those things happening to me at that moment as best I could. I connected to how it would feel in my body to be enjoying the things I saw for my life. I even played my affirmations in my car while I drove.

I still do this! My kids laugh, and they think that their mother is crazy, but that's okay with me. I know that they are sponges and one day will be saying their own affirmations.

> To manifest that which you desire,
> you need to speak the language of your
> body—your emotions.

I began to shift all my words of lack to the affirmative. I used to say, "I am alone, I want a partner, I want to find my purpose . . ."

Now I say, "I am always surrounded by those I love. I have all the passion and love I seek, I make a difference in the world, I change people's lives through my writing . . ."

Huge difference, right?

As a child, I was taught to ask the Universe for the things that I wanted in my life. But people all over the world would tell you that they pray and do not get what they prayed for. Why is that?

Here is the important piece that makes the puzzle work. The Universe is a mirror. It mirrors your emotions and your state of mind. Wisdom teacher Gregg Braden wisely points out: "The field provides us with a reflection, an outer mirror of our inner experiences. The Universe serves as feedback mechanism of sorts. In that mirror, we can see our true beliefs—not just what we like to think we believe."[8]

Have you ever noticed that some people are in a perpetual state of bad luck and misery, while others seem to get lucky every time? If you constantly live in a state of lack and a state of discontent, the Universe captures that and mirrors those states and emotions back to you.

Attraction is simply what we are putting out as waves of energy and what we are attracting back to us with our thoughts and emotions. Again, this phenomenon goes back to the first fundamental truth that I told you about. *You create everything that you experience.* Yes, even the things that hurt you. If you believe that life is lonely and difficult, for instance, well then, that is what you will find happening in your world.

The worst part is that many people are unconscious of the true power they have.

The Power of Affirmative Prayer and Gratitude

You are a powerhouse of magnetic energy, electrical transmitters. Your every thought transmits signals that are then interpreted into the universal field of possibilities and you get what you think about. Braden encourages taking responsibility for ourselves, saying: "If you want to manifest great things in life, then it rests solely on your ability to *become* these qualities you want in each moment of every day. We must *embody* in our lives every condition that we wish to experience in our world."[9] The key puzzle piece to asking the Universe is NOT in the asking, but in the affirmation and gratitude that you already have it.

In his book *Secrets of the Lost Mode of Prayer*, Braden describes accompanying his Native American friend David, a rainmaker, to pray in the desert near his home in northern New Mexico during a drought. He was surprised when David took off his shoes and gently placed his feet on the dried ground and closed his eyes. After only a few moments, David took a deep breath and said, "Let's go. Our work is finished here."[10]

Confused, Braden tells David that he thought he was going to pray for rain. David laughs and answers, "I said that I would pray rain. If I had prayed 'for' rain, it would never happen. The key is that when you ask for something to happen, you give power to what you do not have. Prayers for healing empower the sickness. Prayers for rain empower the drought."[11]

Amazingly simple, don't you think, yet a perspective so foreign to us? David prayed in the *feeling* that what he wanted to see was already there. When he took off his shoes and put his feet on the ground, he felt what it would feel like to have his face wet from the fresh rain and his feet deepened in the mud from the wet ground due to so much rain. He then made sure to express gratitude for receiving the rain.

This is the key to making our prayers and affirmations materialize. I was shocked at how something so simple is so absent from our knowledge.

> Don't dream your life,
> live your dream.[12]
> —Mark Twain

Let me recap, so that you cannot fail to understand it.

Affirmations and prayers need to be in the present as already materialized things. You must invoke the feeling, the emotions, of what you would feel like if you had those things already in your life and give gratitude for having them.

I started to do the same as David did with my prayers and affirmations. I began to live in the feeling of having the things that were important to me. I would fall asleep each night in a state of meditation, which has become my form of prayer, and envisioning what it would feel like to have this book in your hands and being read by millions of people. I felt my message changing lives. Each night I would envision words flowing through my hands and forming the precise message that I was to convey in this book to you. I felt myself being guided by a divine force even before I could conceive of it.

Your Destiny Lies in Your Thoughts

Here's a way to understand this through the lens of brain science. "You connect to your destiny in your thoughts. It's a process of mental rehearsal practicing living in that future on the daily basis and feeling and living in the emotion. Your brain cannot distinguish the difference between an experience taking place outside of us, or one being created by thought alone. Consequently, to the brain, this experience has already happened."[13]

Since we can create and manifest by thought alone, I began to see, feel, smell, and rejoice that you are holding the very book that you are reading right now. I envisioned myself admiring its cover and having an overwhelming sense of gratitude to the Universe for guiding me in birthing my dream. The fact you are reading this right now, means my thoughts, emotions, and intentions have indeed manifested.

The more I learned, the more fascinated I became. I was learning so much. I was making new brain connections. I kept joking telling my kids that I was learning and evolving so much that I was soon going to be floating. I simply could not get enough. I felt in my soul that this was my time to learn and prepare for my destined journey.

THIRTEEN

....

THE LAW OF ATTRACTION

*"You attract what YOU ARE not what YOU WANT. If you
want to be great, then be great."*
—*Kushandwizdom blog*

Wayne Dyer's books, *The Power of Intention* and *Wishes Fulfilled* became one of my night table bibles. Calling "those things which do not exist as though they did"[1] (Romans 4:17) became my daily focus.

These books taught me that I could call unto a higher power to connect to the quantum field of possibilities. This field is easily available to any of us if we choose to claim it. The key ingredient to this, however, is not just to imagine what we want but to feel it. A dream without intention, emotion, and action becomes nothing more than a daydream. That is why so many of us say affirmations or pray all day long, yet nothing ever happens.

The Power of Emotion

Same as it is when saying affirmations or prayers, the most powerful ingredient in manifesting is emotion. Emotion is the language of the body and heart, and the heart generates the most powerful magnetic field there is in the body. Feeling the emotion of that which you desire as if it has already happened, even before it materializes, is the key to manifestation. That is why Gregg Braden's friend David, at the time of calling rain in his prayer, engaged all his senses: feeling the rain in his face, smelling the smell of it, seeing the ground wet, and feeling his feet standing in the mud.

Feeling the emotion of that which you desire as if it has already happened, even before it materializes, is the key to manifestation.

Another way of understanding this concept is in harnessing what Joe Dispenza calls the model of causing an effect (as opposed to the older model known as cause *and* effect). I love how he says, "You can't wait for your wealth to feel abundant. You can't wait for your healing to feel wholeness. You can't wait for your new relationship to feel love. You can't wait for your success to feel empowered. You can't wait for a mystical moment to feel in awe of life. That's the old model of cause-and-effect, waiting for something outside of us to give us relief from the lack and separation we feel inside of us."[2]

He is advocating the same thing as other spiritual teachers but using a more empirical, science-based approach to the mechanics of our brain and its power. The underlying truth is the same: We can't make things manifest in our lives by waiting or wanting them to come externally. The secret to having your prayers heard and materialized is in LIVING THE EFFECT FIRST!

As Dispenza says: "We need to move from cause and effect to causing an effect. It means the moment you start to feel abundant, your wealth is coming. When you start to feel whole, you begin to heal. The moment you feel empowered, you will lean toward success. The moment you are in love with yourself and life, you will magnetize an equal. The moment you are in awe of life, is the moment the mystical blesses you. That's causing an effect."[3]

The Power of Worthiness

The second key of manifesting is believing you deserve it, that you are worthy of receiving your desires and being grateful for cocreating them. People often do a good job of going through the steps of a manifesting exercise, yet nothing happens. This is likely because they are saying one thing in the conscious mind, but in the subconscious mind they have some limiting beliefs they are not aware they have. Their mind chatter contradicts what they expect. And, of course, the Universe could also be blocking manifestation if there is something better and greater for us. But we need to be sure we are deliberately attempting to clear our own blocks too.

If you are trying to manifest the love of your life, yet at a deep, subconscious level you have programmed your mind to think and feel that you do not deserve to have someone to love, what do you think will manifest? Nothing! No one! Becoming aware of the limiting chatter emanating from the recesses of your own mind is crucial. Do this so that you can establish your worthiness to receive in your conscious and subconscious minds. This is the ultimate manifesting key.

Neville Goddard writes: "You are consciousness. You are the creator. This is the mystery; this is the great secret known by the seers, prophets, and mystics throughout the ages. This is the truth that you can never know intellectually. . . . The important thing is that it is within you, it is you, and it is your world."[4] What he is saying is that because you are God you are worthy of manifesting anything that is in alignment with your highest and greatest good.

The Power of Time and Space

The last ingredient that I learned for manifesting is not attaching to the outcome. You must be willing to let go of your timelines for things to arrive so that the Universe can have a chance to do her work. Sometimes we are so impatient to see the world as we want it to be that we try to control things, and, in doing so, block the flow of the Universe.

We ourselves too often block our opportunities and impede the miracles that would otherwise filter through our lives. As 12th-century Persian Muslim Shams-i-Tabrizi, who was the poet Rumi's spiritual instructor, describes this phenomenon: "When I run after what I think I want, my days are a furnace of stress and anxiety. If I sit in my own place of patience, what I need and want flows to me and without pain."[5]

So, don't attached to the outcome. If something is meant for your highest good, it will simply flow to you. If it does not, then have the patience that your path will be revealed in its right time. This does not mean you should do nothing. Of course not. You hold your intention. You make decisions based on where you are going, not on where you are. You then step back and let the Universe do her job of working out *how* things can come to you.

I became intrigued by this process. I made a "mind movie," a powerful visualization tool, which is basically a three-minute movie containing snapshots symbolizing what I want for my perfect life. Making this film allowed me to connect my emotions to pictures so that I could view them in the now whenever I wanted. I added affirmations and a soundtrack to this film that inspired my soul and facilitated me in connecting with the future I was envisioning.

Generally, I would watch my mind movie after I had spent many hours in meditation working to define an architectural blueprint for the life that I felt I was worthy of having. As a result, today in my mind I have already spent countless afternoons taking walks on my favorite beach and seeing magnificent sunsets and nights lit by incredible moons, as well as holding the hand of the man I love even though, as of this writing, he has not yet materialized in my life. I trust that he is already on his way!

I have envisioned myself talking to you and large groups of people about the power of intention and personal transformation. I have spent time in dimensions I did not know existed until recently, feeling emotions in my body, crying tears of joy, and living the life I desire, which I am now happy to say I am currently manifesting in the material realm.

FOURTEEN

....

MINDFULNESS

"You have to accept, believe, and surrender."
—Joe Dispenza

In the last several years, I have learned to be aware of my subconscious thoughts. This is a stage of consciousness that Joe Dispenza terms *getting beyond yourself.*[1] Transformation happens only when you are aware of your behavior; because then you can decide which are the parts of your programs that you want to retire. You are the architect of your future.

Having this new knowledge empowered me. I no longer felt like an actor on a stage. Rather, I felt like the director of the play I was starring in. Every day, I woke up with a conscious intent to be the best person I could be.

True change comes when we stop being defined by our memories and experiences of the past. True change comes when we willfully practice focusing our energy daily on learning new things and experiencing new emotions, new more empowering thoughts, and new events. "When you become aware of the emotions of the past and you begin to retire the old self neurologically, biologically, and genetically, you being to create a new self."[2]

Over a few years, I went from being in a constant unhealthy state of stress, contraction, fear, and survival to being in a healthy state of homeostasis. I shifted my thoughts. I began to create an emotional reality that was rooted in my experiences of gratitude, love, wholeness, and acceptance. I repeated living in these emotions on a daily basis.

It was true what Dispenza says: "When you can hold an image of your desire in your mind, the thought in your mind becomes the experience and the end product of an experience is an emotion. When you're in the present moment inspired and embracing the future, the brain doesn't know the difference between an experience happening inside your brain by thought alone, and an experience happening outside of you."[3]

When your body essentially becomes your mind and you are no longer falling victim to the limiting fearful thoughts of the past, you are free to begin to consider the possibilities from the quantum field. That is when you begin to embrace a new reality even before it manifests. This kind of shift in my matrix resulted in a change in my personal vibration. My mind went from feeling separate from my body to feeling connected and synchronized to my soul.

The things I was learning and experiencing were magnificent. *How was it that I went through life so unconsciously before now?* I would ask myself. Each day I woke up sensing in a new way that my every step was being guided by a cosmic presence. I was no longer in control, nor did I care to be. I became extremely sensitive to the Universe's guidance and the directions that were being presented.

I felt connected to the quantum field of possibilities, and let me tell you, the most amazing thing about being connected is that when you feel whole, at peace, and complete with the life you have, there is no room for wanting.

One of the things I learned was to live in a state of mindfulness. Among other things, I started to pay attention to life: to really see, to really hear, and to really appreciate all the little things that would be so easy to take for granted. As part of my new spiritual practice, I made it a daily habit to notice something I had formerly taken for granted and I found myself falling in love with nature. Noticing the green leaves on a tree, I would be drawn to touch and connect with them.

Trees are alive just like us, and they feel and hear too. A couple of the trees behind my house were dying when I moved in. Their leaves were looking unseasonably brown. I began to talk to them each day and told them how grateful I was for them, that I needed them, and that I knew their health could be restored. Within two weeks of doing this every day, those trees grew new leaves and became even more beautiful than before.

Because of my new mindfulness, I was able to experience the wonder of the trees returning to robust health day by day—missing none of the subtle nuances.

As I healed and became more mindful, I felt a strong urge to connect directly with the earth, so I would walk barefoot routinely to ground myself in the soil. There are many benefits of earthing or grounding yourself. It helps with immune response, recharges you and even heals you. There is a park right next to the exit where I would pick up my daughter from the subway after school. I would go a few minutes early, just so I could take off my shoes and walk on the grass. My connection to the earth centered me. While I was in the park, I would close my eyes and make a point of listening to the sounds of the birds and feeling the brush of the wind on my face and the rays of the sun warming my skin. I had never previously been able to feel so much from such simple sensations. It was as if I had finally broken free from the mental chains of my unhappiness that had numbed me. It was as if I was seeing, feeling, and experiencing life for the first time. And life was vibrant.

> Being present is the most important thing you can do because the present moment is the only time you have.

Being present is the most important thing you can do for yourself and others because the present moment is the only time you have. The best gift you can give those you love is being fully present with them. The best gift you can give yourself is being in the moment without worrying about things you can't control—like the past and the future. Focusing on past or future simply robs you of the happiness you could be experiencing by staying focused in the now.

Don't live on autopilot. Be mindful of the things happening around you. Stop for a moment periodically and notice the sky and its puffy clouds. When I was a kid (and I am sure you did this too), I would lie on the grass and look for all the amazing images I could discern in the clouds. When was the last time you did this?

Close your eyes on a sunny day and feel the warmth on your face. Look people in the eyes when they talk. Don't just hear your children when they talk, listen.

Next time you hold your partner's hand, feel the sensation of his or her touch, feel the texture of his or her skin, and the temperature.

Kiss with your eyes closed and kiss deeply.

During the next three breaths you take, right after reading this page, gift your lungs with slow, deep breaths. Doesn't that feel amazing?

When was the last time you went out at night to gaze at the moon or watched the changing colors of the sky in the late afternoon when the sun is going down? We are all guilty of going through our days unaware. We miss all the beauty. Break the habit. It's tragic we often only appreciate and notice things once they have passed, once they are gone, once they have died. Without mindfulness, it's easy to go through life without noticing the grandeur of our planet.

FIFTEEN

······································

AYAHUASCA

"I can be hurt by nothing but my thoughts."
—*A Course in Miracles*

Four years ago, when my emotions were at rock bottom, I suffered from a chronic irritation in my body that did not allow me to have a normal life. This irritation started during my abusive relationship when the man I loved began his dance of leaving and coming back to me. I do not want to go into every detail of the condition; it's sufficient to say that the irritation was in my reproductive system. Despite seeing three of the top gynecologists in Toronto and undergoing every test known to them, there was no cure for what I had. I also went to Nicaragua to see the top gynecologist there, and after many more tests, still came out with no precise answer for what I had. It was not contagious. But it did not register on any of their conventional tests. They performed repeated colposcopies and the biopsies were all normal, yet the specialists were baffled as they could see at first glance the severe irritation on my skin.

These specialists were simply testing and guessing, throwing darts at a dartboard to see what would stick. They had me on numerous drugs and were looking for answers simply by going through a process of elimination. I was sent to the pelvic and pain management clinic where more tests were done, more medications were thrown at me, and all the doctors were trying to address the symptoms without ever bothering to address the root cause of my condition—which I'll tell you right now was stress from the subconscious beliefs I had about abandonment. My body knew before my mind did that I needed to get out of the toxic relationship and wake up.

Eventually, I was on so many different medications and steroids that I felt like a walking pharmacy. Medication was not helping me, but it was creating terrible side effects. One of the medications would make me jump in my sleep constantly. It was funny and crazy at the same time. The minute my body would sense my eyes closing, the jumps would start. I knew that it was the meds because I did not have that issue before then. As soon as I stopped taking that drug, the jumping stopped as well.

Other drugs made me gain a lot of weight, retain water, affected my mood, and even suspended my period for about two and half years. Nothing reduced the irritation. I started to believe that the illness was never going to let me lead a normal life again.

Discouraged by conventional medicine, I ventured to the jungles of Peru to do an Ayahuasca retreat. Ayahuasca is a healing plant that grows exclusively in the Amazonian basin. Its name means "vine of the soul." When combined with another plant, chacruna, which contains high levels of dimethyltryptamine (DMT), it becomes a powerful psychedelic. The local shamans, descendants of the ancient Incas, make a brew out of these plants, which they have used as a medicine for thousands of years, to alter their state of consciousness and connect to the spirt world. Having thoroughly researched this magnificent healing plant, I went to Peru in the hopes that the brew could heal me emotionally, spiritually, and physically. It was an incredible journey and one of the scariest experiences I have ever had.

I had been hearing about Ayahuasca for a few years from others in my spiritual circles. Countless testimonies from seekers spoke about its remarkable, "magical" healing properties. The plant is said to cleanse all the negative energy trapped in the body through a process of purging. It has become increasingly popular in the western world due to its ability to support the healing of addiction, depression, post-traumatic stress, and anxiety.

More than anything, Ayahuasca makes you face your shadow (the parts of your psyche that you have repressed) and every mental demon you have hidden comes out. Through visions that are unique to the individual, Ayahuasca brings to the surface all the things that you need to heal in your life. This is similar to the exploration I did of my childhood imprints through another means.

So, there I was, alone, thousands of miles from home on a boat on the Amazon River, traveling into the jungle to heal my soul. It was surreal. As the night falls, the jungle comes alive. I could hear every creature and reptilian sound and my only companion was the beautiful reflection of the moon staring at me so perfectly painted on the calm waters of the river. I stood still, in awe at the immensity of the environment, listening to the sound of bats flapping their wings and inhaling the lingering sweet smell of *mapacho,* my shaman's favorite sacred tobacco.

After five Ayahuasca ceremonies done on that trip brought me incredible revelations, visions, and insights, I returned home feeling better. I had relief, but it was only temporary. A few months later, the symptoms returned, and I did not know why. I was not as aware of the root causes as I am today, and yet, having had some success in the jungle, I felt encouraged. I knew I was on to something, something that had to do with my energy and internal balance, but I didn't know to what extent my symptoms were being caused by my mind and emotions.

I did not stop my search for spiritual healing. I visited energy healers. After three years of enduring every medical examination my conventional doctors had in their arsenal, I was convinced that my problem was metaphysical. I had some blocked energy that was manifesting in my body as these symptoms. I knew from the work that I had done with a naturopath that every disease exists at a certain frequency in our bodies.

I, and I alone, had the power to heal whatever had manifested in my own body.

According to chiropractor Darren Weissman, "At the core of every symptom, every stress, every disease pattern that we experience, whether it be physical or emotional, there are emotions and memories that are buried in our subconscious mind and when these are triggered, our body reacts manifesting what it is feeling in different parts of our body."[1] And like Weissman, Joe Dispenza believes that diseases manifest when our energy is out of alignment over a prolonged period of time. However, the piece I was missing was that I, and I alone, had the power to heal whatever had manifested in my own body.

What Ayahuasca taught me was that for too long I had been focused on finding the cure, the relief, and the healing I needed from external sources. Now I trusted myself more.

SIXTEEN

·····································

CHANGE YOUR MIND,
HEAL YOUR LIFE

"Lose what needs to be lost to find what needs to be found."
—E-motion

The piece I was missing to heal my body finally came to me through the work of Joe Dispenza. I remember hearing him talk about sickness for the first time in a video. He said, "If you think of a disease logically, where does it begin? It begins inside of us. Why then would you look to something outside of yourself to heal it?"[1]

This remark spoke to me. It was an awakening call. What he said was common sense, and I became intrigued, so I ordered his book *You Are the Placebo*. From that moment forward, I began to learn everything that I could from him about how to go inward to change my subconscious programming and heal my body. I enrolled in Dispenza's online courses and attended many of his live workshops. From my studies, I understood that it did not matter how much medications a specialist would put me on; it was not going to make me better because I was not yet addressing the things that were causing my symptoms.

It did not matter how many naturopaths I saw, how much Ayahuasca I drank or how many energy healers worked on me. I would get only temporary relief until I reprogrammed my subconscious mind. The truth was that even with all the medications I had never really believed it possible that I was going to get cured. I needed to change the beliefs like this one that were making me feel unhappy and sick.

Ayahuasca healed me temporarily. Energy healers would unblock my stuck energy temporarily. But the minute I was left to my own devices I always went back to being my old self with all my fearful and angry thoughts, limiting beliefs, and flooding my body with the same unhealthy cocktail of emotions day after day. So, what should I have expected was going to happen? The illness persisted because I kept recreating it and giving it a perfect environment in which to thrive!

Even though I really did want to change and heal, neither my brain nor my body could change as long as I continued to be controlled by negative emotions. As Dispenza writes: "Most diseases are caused by stress related conditions, and when our bodies experience stress for extended periods of time, it moves out of homeostasis—the ideal state of internal balance and equilibrium."[2]

You may recall that there was a time in my life when I was fully disconnected, charged with negative emotions, limiting beliefs, and heart-dissolution, and I felt like I had no purpose. This state of being constituted a prolonged period of stress that threw my body completely out of balance. Then, I was reinforcing the disease over and over by living in a present based on my perceptions and angry experiences from the past. So, I and I alone was responsible for manufacturing the illness my body was expressing. Again, the first fundamental truth I have been telling you about is that we attract everything we face in our lives. By living constantly immersed in the biochemistry of the emotions of stress, self-judgment, and guilt, I was keeping my body sick without any hope for healing.

"You can think positively all you want, but the 5 percent of your mind that's conscious will feel as if it's swimming upstream against the current of the other 95 percent of your mind which has hardwired the negative memories you've been harboring for the past 35 years of your life. Your body and mind are working in opposition. No wonder you don't get very far when you try to fight the current."[3]

The mind is incredibly powerful. We can heal by thought alone, a phenomenon known as the *placebo effect*. We also can get sick by thought alone. Which do you think I chose?

If you are not familiar with the placebo effect, let me take a moment to describe it to you. This effect was originally observed during controlled experiments to test the efficacy of new drugs or surgical procedures. Some people get better simply because they are made to believe that they are being given a real treatment, but unbeknown to them they are actually receiving either a sugar pill, saline solution, or a false surgery.

According to Dispenza, these people feel better because they surrender to the idea that the treatment they are taking is going to make them better. When they see the pill or undergo the surgery (whatever the treatment entails), they associate hope and possibility with the treatment. Therefore, they develop positive emotions for the treatment. As they put trust and energy in the drug (or procedure), they begin to heal completely through their thought alone. Dispenza explains it this way: "People start to think new thoughts and connect to the possibility of getting healed that they begin to program their autonomic nervous system to make their own pharmacy of chemicals that matches the exact same chemicals or treatment they think they are getting.[4]

Placebo effect is the cause of the cure when it is clear that there is no way it is the drug or external stimulus that is doing the healing. It is your body, through the power of your consistent thoughts of getting better that is doing the healing. In other words, we alone often can be our own best drugs, healers, and placebos because healing takes place inside the body—not outside it.

I love the story Dispenza tells in *You Are the Placebo* about a man who died after being told he had cancer, even though an autopsy later revealed he'd been misdiagnosed. He had no traces of cancer, yet his constant stress over the thought of it, led him to his death. My takeaway from this is that our brains are so powerful that they can convince us of things that are not real, so we must beware the power of anticipation.

Something funny happened to me that illustrates the power of anticipation. I was in my car driving when I received a phone call from my daughter's school. They had been checking the kids in her class for lice and found some eggs on her head, so they asked me to pick her up and get her treated. Apparently after the March break that year, more than half the class had lice! As I hung up the phone, I began to scratch my head. I could not stop. I could feel things crawling in my scalp. As soon as I picked her up, we went straight to the lice-squad clinic to get her de-liced. On the way there, I was feeling even worse. I had the sensation of all kinds of tiny critters crawling on my skull. I was convinced, through the power of autosuggestion, that I too had lice. But when I got my hair looked at, I was clean as a whistle.

Once it became clear to me that in order to heal my illness and my life I had to cleanse myself of every negative emotion that I had been living with during the first part of my life, especially the ones I had immersed myself in for the past decade. I had to peel the onion to get beyond its layers to the true root cause of my unhappiness. *That is a lot of peeling,* I thought to myself.

Luckily, I had become so much more aware of my thoughts by this point and done so much work on discovering my childhood patterns that I was ready to unlearn the ideas that were making me sick. I had to release old energy from my body and mind in order to make room for new energy and new possibilities.

Everything we manifest in our lives daily is rooted in the brain. Our bodies and minds are connected in such a way that as we change our minds and practice living in a new reality, we can change and heal our bodies. Changing how we think about ourselves and the things around us so that our thoughts are more healthful is as important to our well-being as breathing clear air is for our lungs. We can't heal if we do not address the quality of our thoughts.

> You can't think greater than you feel.[5]
> —Joe Dispenza

By now you have heard me say over and over that our thoughts and feelings are powerful and how we think and feel has a direct impact on our biology, chemistry, and physiology. Science has even proven that we no longer need to be defined by our genes because we can alter our genetic expression. This makes us ultimately responsible for who we are—we can no longer blame our lives and well-being on our parentage. We are not victims.

Knowing that you, and you alone, possess the power to choose the genes that you want to turn on and turn off, how do you feel? Empowered?

It's all up to you. You are the architect and the creator, remember?

Once it became crystal clear to me that I was making myself sick by blocking my body's ability to regenerate and heal itself I realized that I was creating the opposite effect of a placebo. I was being a *nocebo*.

But the news was not all bad. Evidently, if my emotions, life, and state of being were making me sick, by changing them I could heal myself too. All I needed to do was shift my state of being to one that was energy-rich and oxygen-rich so that the DNA in my genes could have the chance to thrive and express themselves fully in the way they were meant to do. Gregg Braden explains how this works on the biomolecular level of the cells in our bodies: "The emotions of joy, contentment, acceptance, appreciation, gratitude in turn make our DNA strands unwind and fully relax in a new vitalized heal state.[6]

With my new education in epigenetics, suddenly I felt superhuman, and as such, I could no longer be defeated. I no longer felt a failure. I no longer felt helpless. I saw that I am powerful enough to influence matter, to influence not only my own body, but with the energy emanating from my body I could influence the entire world. What my spiritual adviser, Sabrina Heartsong, told me at the start of my healing journey now made sense. She had told me that I did not have to worry about changing the world. All I needed to worry about was changing myself. That by simply changing my vibration, I could make a positive impact on the planet.

Understanding the depths of my power to transmit energy and to heal was an eye opener for me. I was disturbed, however, when I considered this information in the light of what I already knew about the subconscious mind: specifically, that the subconscious mind, which accounts for 95 percent of our mental activity, is running loose on autopilot.

If thinking the same thoughts leads to taking the same actions and feeling the same emotions day after day, what was I to do to change my thought patterns? That was my question.

I did not want to be stuck living in the same narrow reality for the rest of my life. I remembered being impressed by reading Wayne Dyer's book *Wishes Fulfilled,* which at the time I had not known could be applied to physical healing. But now I realized it could be! He said: "If you want to elevate your life and become a *manifestor,* then you have to change what you've believed to be true about yourself that has landed you where you are."[7]

One day, after a year of literally working on myself every second, I finally felt ready and strong enough to make a promise to myself right in front of the mirror. That day, I decided that I was going to eliminate any version of who I had been programmed to be that did not resonate with my soul. I was willing to let the victim persona in me die once and for all. I swore to let go of any thought, memory, emotion, and subconscious program I had created that negatively impacted me. I felt motivated by my absolute certainty that I could change, shift, and transform. My time had come.

That day, I promised myself that even if I had to sit in my fear and endure the discomfort of any anxious thoughts that came from stepping into the unknown, I finally was going to be the person I had been born to be. It was an incredibly powerful moment for me, one that had such intensity in it that it could overcome my emotional conditioning.

Transformation is achieved when the pain of being yourself is greater than your fear of looking inward. Change is achieved when the energy attached to your current desire for change is greater than the comfort of staying in the known reality of your old self.

Joe Dispenza explains: "When you are strong enough to restrain the chatter of your mind which tries to get you back in the comfort of your old self and you keep reinforcing the new thoughts, these new thoughts eventually become the strongest signal in your brain. The old connections are replaced and you begin to create new circuits of neurons in your brain and a new self begins to emerge."[8] It was this process, my friend, along with all the other tools I have previously mentioned, that helped my soul finally transform.

Since making that decision on that day, I have made peace with my demons, I have made peace with food and my body, I have made peace with my past, and more importantly, I have finally learned to accept and love who I am at any given moment. I have let go of all the old versions of myself and all the people that were not serving my highest good.

In the process, I learned that I did not need to be any of those versions I had created to be someone. I WAS ALREADY SOMEONE. A huge sense of freedom came with this realization and my acceptance of myself.

I went to every layer, every emotion, every thought, and every experience that made up my past and present and began to transform each of them. I called them by name. Each time I caught myself reacting to something in my present that was overlaid on a past memory and experience, I called it by name and replaced it with an empowering alternative.

I pruned my limiting and unfounded beliefs of the past and sprouted new emotions of love, acceptance, empathy, and gratitude toward myself. This placed me in an elevated state, which when practiced on the daily basis produces new emotions, new behavior, new genetic expression, and new brain cells and neural connections.

I went from experiencing illnesses in my body to feeling vitality, growth, and repair. I stopped suffering from the chronic irritation that I was experiencing because I learned to free myself from all the emotions and trapped energy in my body that were being caused by living in my past.

SEVENTEEN

....

GRATITUDE

*"Nothing new can come into your life unless you are
grateful for what you already have."*
—Michael Bernard Beckwith

E very night, you should leave your slippers far enough under the bed so that when you wake up you need to get down on your knees to reach them. And while you're down there, take a moment to say a small prayer of gratitude. If getting down on your knees is not your thing, take this as a recommendation to spend a bit of time each day being thankful for all that you have in your life. Remember that what you focus on every day is what expands in your life. It's a request to the Universe. If you feel, show, and express gratitude, the Universe will give you more of the same in return.

Starting my day in a state of gratitude was the single most important thing I have ever done to transform my life. Spending even a few minutes in gratitude improved everything. This practice is the fastest way to feel happier and at peace. It boosts the immune system and leads to the formation of new neurological connections in the brain.[1] The repeated act of expressing gratitude will signal to your brain that you are in a creative mode of being, and that's when you begin to heal your body and life such that you can build a future of possibilities.

Starting my day in a state of gratitude was the single most important thing I have ever done to transform my life.

In the film *E-motion*, Neale Donald Walsch tells a wonderful story about a husband's advice to his wife on his deathbed. Being able from this perspective to discern what is important in life, he says, "Come close. I don't have much time left. Remember this each morning, the moment you take your head off the pillow: You already have all you need."[2]

Hearing this story made me think a lot, and I took it to heart.

Each morning now, as part of my spiritual practice, I make a point to become conscious of all the things I have in my life that are amazing. Before my feet hit the floor, I make sure I have expressed my gratitude for all I have—and not just for the good. I give thanks for the lessons, such as an illness that comes to warn me if I need to pay attention to something that is throwing me off balance. I express my gratitude for the big things and the little things.

To live in a state of perpetual gratitude, you must practice being grateful for all the different elements that make up the human experience. It is easy to feel happy and grateful when things are going according to plan. But that is not how it truly works in your favor. You need to feel grateful for it all—the pain, the grief, the loss, the love, the fortune, and the misfortune.

Too many people live unhappy lives feeling like victims of the environment. Being in a state of gratitude means that you accept the beautiful sunny days and the cloudy days. Take responsibility. If you do not like what you are creating, including an attitude or a perception, change it. As Joe Dispenza says: "You can learn and change in a state of pain and suffering, or you learn and change in a state of joy and inspiration."[3] The choice of how you feel is yours.

The beautiful thing is that we are gifted each day with a new tomorrow, a chance to make a new start. It is in that assurance of tomorrow that we humans find this world worth living. Everything passes. That is guaranteed. The night is always followed by daylight. Thunder and rain give way for rainbows. From knowing this, we obtain hope and strength to endure our lows.

My great grandmother used to tell me the story of a king who had a wise man among his advisors. One day, on the king's birthday, the wise man gave the king a gift: two small boxes wrapped in beautiful silverleaf paper. The wise man told his king, *"Open the first box when you feel you have reached all the happiness you could ever wish for. Open the second box when you think you are grieving so much that you cannot go on anymore."*

Years passed. There came a time when the king felt he was the most fortunate man the earth had ever known. He remembered the words of his trusted adviser and proceeded to open the first box. Inside there was a small piece of paper that read: *"This too shall pass!"*

Years and years later, the king had aged and fallen ill, he had lost his queen, his adult daughter had moved away, and he had lost most of his fortune. He felt depressed and considered himself the most unfortunate man in the world. He proceeded to open the second box. Inside there was a small piece of paper that read: *"This too shall pass!"*

That is life: All the good, the happy, the bad, and the sad eventually pass. You must not waste your happy times worrying about the not-so-good times that can come. Enjoy what you have at any given moment because, as the story illustrates, this too shall pass.

When you learn not only to think grateful thoughts occasionally, but to express gratitude daily, your hope and your faith will become hardwired into your subconscious mind. If you can achieve that, nothing will stop you. To borrow another insightful line I've heard said repeatedly, you may find yourselves in situations where you are cracked open, but you'll never be broken.

With daily practice, I shifted all my focus from the fear and anger that I was feeling and focused instead on love and gratitude. I began to breathe deeply and opened myself to appreciate the things I had and paid less attention to the ones I was lacking.

Try it. What do you have to lose? You possibly have everything to gain.

Living in a state of gratitude felt strange for me in the beginning. I was so programmed to focus just on the negative; but I pushed myself and gave thanks at first for obvious things like my kids, my family, my health, my financial wellbeing, and my friends. As time went by, I noticed that it had become easier to think of a myriad of things to be thankful for. There were mornings when I couldn't stop because I had so much to appreciate.

I took a workshop with happiness "guru" Shawn Achor and he recommended saying three unique things you are grateful for over a 30-day period without repeating the same things twice. While I did not follow that exact format, I see how this would be a very good exercise to get your mind used to noticing new things that enrich your life. If you want, try it.

It is easy for people to feel grateful when things are good. But I find that it is equally important, if not more important, to give gratitude when things are not as good. Remember, you cannot appreciate the light unless you have seen darkness. You cannot appreciate joy without experiencing sorrow, health without sickness, love without loss, abundance without lack.

I had a beautiful gratitude experience once. I was in my daughter's room, falling asleep on her bed in the middle of the day, and I decided to take a moment to express my gratitude in my mind. The feeling was so intense that tears were pouring out of my eyes. I was asleep for a period of two hours, and I don't believe I stopped giving thanks even in my sleep. I could sense that I had stayed in a state of gratitude because as I woke up I was still giving thanks for everything around me and in my life.

You might be shocked at how many things we should be thankful for—especially the invisible things we are likely to take for granted. For example, we should be thankful for every organ in our body that regenerates out of our sight. Speaking for myself, I have discovered that I am inclined always to give thanks to my heart. I feel deep gratitude and awe for its function, for its strength, for its intelligence, for its guidance, and for never steering me in the wrong direction.

Emotions felt in the heart produce magnetic waves that are more powerful than those produced by any other organ in the body. These waves connect us with everything on the planet. Gregg Braden, who has written extensively on the capacity of the heart, says: "The human heart is the strongest generator of both electrical and magnetic fields with the power to influence the very field of this planet, including everything that sustains life and sustains the healing in our bodies."[4] From Braden I learned about the sensory neurites, which are cells in the heart that act like brain cells—but think independently of the brain.[5]

Have you ever heard the expression, "Just listen to your heart! Your heart always knows?" That is because it really does! If I need to make a life-impacting decision, I have learned to ask my heart and trust it's guidance. In the past, I let my brain guide my life. Now, if I cannot get my brain and heart to be in alignment with one another, I follow my heart. It seems to know much faster than my brain what the right thing is for me to do in the moment because the heart doesn't go through filters.

The best way to live is in having constant communication with the heart and viewing the world from a place of gratitude.

I believe the best way to live is in having constant communication with the heart and viewing the world from a place of gratitude. If you do that, nothing will defeat you. You will be strong enough to face the setbacks and circumstances that come. You will learn and grow each time from your pain as you search for the gifted lessons it brings. If a person comes into your life and leaves—well, that person was never meant to play a permanent role in your life.

Find something that makes you want to get up in the morning, something bigger than yourself. This too can inspire gratitude. I find that leading a life of service to others does it for me. Find something that makes your life on earth worth living. When you feel grateful, there is no room for lack. When you are in love with life, it is impossible to feel down and sad.

When you feel whole and grateful for who you are and what you have at any given moment in your life, that's when the miracles happen. Because you are connected to a field of infinite possibilities, as you show gratitude, the Universe manifests the best outcomes for you.

Start today. Don't wait a second longer. Embrace whatever pain or circumstance you are going through now. Close your eyes. Sit still and in silence and let the Universe guide you. Don't try to control it. Whatever pain or problem you may think you have, don't fight it, don't judge it. It is there for a reason. It is in this pain that your humanity is reinstated. When you can find something in the pain to be grateful for, you begin to heal and to modify your destiny.

When you feel whole and grateful for who you are and what you have at any given moment in your life, that's when the miracles happen.

EIGHTEEN

....

FROM VICTIM TO ARCHITECT

*"Your life does not get better by chance, it gets
better by change."*
—Jim Rohn

O nce I focused on creation, I no longer had time
to feel sorry for myself or to feel miserable
about things that I was lacking. It is true what
the spiritual teachers say: "Where your attention goes,
your energy flows."

At the beginning of my journey I had done everything
I could to source happiness outside myself. But once I
was no longer being ruled by the stress hormones in my
body I was freed of the need to find something to ame-
liorate my pain. I finally had enough energy to envision
and create the life that I wanted. Months later I discovered that I was no longer missing the usual external

stimuli to get my "high" of happiness. I was getting my high internally from simply living in the feelings of gratitude, appreciation, oneness, wholeness, and aliveness in the face of all the incredible possibilities that I could sense for my life and my children.

Your energy field is generated by your current state of being. Consequently, my new state of being established a new vibrational blueprint that was radiating into the Universe. By operating in a state associated with high-frequency emotions, such as love, gratitude, joy, peace, empathy, forgiveness, I began attracting these exact things into my life.

We are magnetic beings. I know that I have been telling you this throughout the book, but it is worth repeating as it is only through repetition that new circuits of neurons wire together. I'm doing my best to help you wire your brain for the same happiness as mine now is!

Everything that I was experiencing seemed to be a miracle. If moments of sadness, fear, or confusion came, they lasted briefly as compared to before. I had the tools to shift my perception and bounce back from feeling blue.

Low-vibration emotions, such as guilt, fear, shame, anger, and insecurity, were left in the past. By revisiting those emotions, I would only attract more of the same and that was something I decided I was no longer willing to allow.

A major turning point in my healing process was when I realized that I felt happy with what I had. I stopped waiting for external things to change how I felt inside. I stopped looking for relationships to assuage my loneliness or rid me of thoughts of feeling unloved. I stopped overeating to suppress my sensation of emptiness. *I birthed the real me, the empowered me, the woman I felt I was always meant to be.*

How did I know that I was making a transformational leap?

I knew that I was evolving when I stopped having a constant feeling of needing something. I woke up one day and I thought, *There is nothing more that I wish to have for my life, other than more of what I already have.* I felt full. Complete. At peace.

It wasn't just my own perception either. People around me noticed that I was different, happier and calmer. A photographer taking my picture one day made the observation that the energy transmitted in the pictures through the lenses was one of absolute resolution and peace. Yes, that is how I was feeling—and still do. I feel happy and I tell that to everyone I meet, especially to myself when we meet at the mirror.

Even as a single woman, I have felt more love and passion than ever in my life. I am in love with who I am becoming. I am now so in love with life, my children, my newfound passion for writing that I am excited to create more of the same. I know that a relationship will come when it is the right time.

Surprisingly I did not need to acquire a single thing more than what I already had to experience a life of joy, peace, and love. In the end, these are the only emotions that last or matter. These are the things that gave me the sense of fullness I lacked until recently.

It was not until I began to surrender all the things that I formerly thought I needed to be happy that I began to enjoy the things I had. It was not until I let go of the life that I thought I should have that I began to live the life I was meant to have. I don't know where my future will take me or who I will be with, but that is not what matters today. Today I have all I need!

If you would like to make peace with your past, you can.

If you would like to make peace with your past in the same way that I made peace with mine, you can. And this is a necessary step if you want to live free from suffering. Living in the past and holding on to resentment and disappointment is a sure way to never achieve peace. Holding on to old hurts will zap the happiness right out of your life.

I love a line that Oprah said in one of the many interviews of her I have watched: "Forgiveness is giving up the hope that the past could have been different."[1]

The past is what it is, my friend. Trust me when I tell you this. Accept what has happened and move on. The negative energy we attached to hurtful events like betrayals does not affect the people we resent. It only poisons us, making us sick and unhappy. Forgiveness is not for those who wrong us. Forgiveness does not mean you excuse poor behaviors. Rather, it's about coming to terms with the fact that you can't change what cannot be changed. All you can do is change yourself. Forgiveness is for you!

The best revenge you can have on someone who has attempted to destroy you is in liberating yourself from the pain and anger that binds you to that person. I was talking to a Jewish friend of mine who went on a trip to visit some of the concentration camps in Poland and Germany a few years ago. I asked her how she could have the stomach to go and see all of that. Her response shocked me. She said, "I go so they can see me, and so they see that they eliminated some of us but could not eliminate all of us. We are still here, strong and growing. We are here to tell the story and to make sure that this happens never again."

Enough said.

So, in the spirit of my Jewish friend, I believe the best revenge on anyone who hurts me is in showing that although they perhaps can crack me, they can never entirely break me.

I don't run from the things that once hurt me. I have learned to find the gifts and lessons in every experience. I no longer avoid pain. I have learned to embrace it, to invite it in to my heart and see the silver lining in the things it presents. I am proud that I found it in my heart to forgive the people who have hurt me intentionally and unintentionally. Every human being, including me and you, is doing the best that he or she can with what he or she knows.

Prince Not-so-Charming did what he did because it was the only way he knew how to be. And I forgave him. This was not to excuse his behavior. It was about me freeing myself from the low frequency of anger and resentment. It is not up to me to change anyone. It is not up to me to avenge or vindicate. The Universe has a set of lessons for each of us. I have mine. He has his. Yours are your own to learn. I am grateful for this painful episode in my life because I would not have been able to find the pieces of myself that I had lost and reclaim them without it.

The quicker you gather up the pieces of your heart, the happier you will be. Make peace with the past, so it does not ruin your present and your future.

Grieve what needs to be grieved.

Mourn what needs to be mourned.

Forgive what needs to be forgiven.

Lose what needs to be lost.

Heal so you can build a bright and inspired future.

AFTERWORD

If you've read this book, it means that I succeeded in my intention to share my journey with you. It means I learned to surrender my life and dreams to the guiding force that helps manifest all my heart's desires. It means I was able to surrender my fears and doubts and rest in the comforting knowledge that the Universe has my back.

Today I am in constant communication with the Universe. I am the architect of my life and, as such, I model for the Universe the things that I want to experience being reflected in the events of my life. The peace in my heart and the vibrancy of my body, which I view as miracles, are the result of the Universe mirroring back to me that which is already in my heart.

Looking back at my life in its entirety brings a smile of gratitude to my face. It is a great feeling to be at peace and appreciate everything I've been through—no matter what it was. I used to look back with regret for the things I'd lost, the things I didn't do, and the things I didn't say. Today I don't regret a single thing. OK, maybe one. I wish I could have started my healing journey a lot sooner.

But even with that, things come when it's their time. Not a moment sooner or later. Everything that has happened to me happened to prepare me for the present moment.

My personal growth mentors were partially correct in advocating that I learn to control my destiny not just by means of hard work or control but by shifting my thoughts and emotions. If the activity of the subconscious mind doesn't match your conscious goals and intentions, then it won't matter how much you work on yourself—you'll always have an internal conflict.

My subconscious programming limited my potential and prevented me from being happy for many years because I truly believed in my limitations. I could not make a difference or alter my circumstances while I continued to believe that I was not good or worthy enough for something else.

I look back with fondness and love at my healing adventures. I especially appreciate my adventure into the Peruvian jungle to visit Mother Ayahuasca (as those who've been touched by her affectionately know her); I thank her for all that she taught me. While that adventure was not where I found my ultimate cure, it is where I relocated my soul. It was there where I had to face my biggest fears, especially my fear of dying. Ayahuasca showed me that I don't need to be afraid of death. More importantly, Ayahuasca taught me not to fear living.

My visions continued to come, revealing incredible things that awaited me in my path. As Mother Ayahuasca so clearly showed me in the visions she granted me, I have a life imbued with only love and gratitude. The most amazing aspect of this journey is the incredible understanding that the Universe and life can only show and give you *that which you have inside.* Remember, you have power in you because God created you that way. All you need to do is claim it.

It is clear in retrospect that my visions propelled me into a spiritual journey of miracles where the only sure thing for me to expect and enjoy is a life of fulfilled wishes.

Do you want to change?

Do you want to learn to be happier?

Then it is so simple. Practice being happy. Practice living immersed in all the emotions you want to experience for your life. Live in the feeling that you already have all that you've ever desired, and you will. This is how you can transform your life. As my teacher Joe Dispenza says: "Go from mind, to body, to soul, from knowledge to experience to wisdom, from thinking to doing to being, to learning it with your head, to practicing with your hands, to knowing it by heart"[1]

My journey of healing and self-discovery may not have been easy, but it was worthwhile. My transformation is far from over, of course. Life is an everlasting process of learning, practice, and evolution. It is a neverending process of exploring new avenues of self-discovery, self-love, and self-compassion. It is not about reaching a certain milestone or destination. It is about being grateful for the journey and the lessons it holds.

I can tell you with certainty that I am no longer living my life unconsciously. I am no longer living life on autopilot. I am awake. I am inspired. I am connected. I am aware. I am committed to a life of expansion. I am committed to being passionate for the gift I am given to be alive. Each new day symbolizes an ability to start life again. I don't want to waste it.

I protect my energy field for my own wellbeing, and for yours. The field of one person affects the fields of every other because we are connected; for this reason, I choose to associate with people who are interested in thriving and being consciously alive. I now know that the present day is the only thing that I have. I know that my past does not equal my future.

I live in a constant state of goodness. My string of little miracles has imbued my life with a sense of mysticism where no matter what comes my way I do not fear. I live with a deep sense of faith that the Universe is forever on guard to protect me and guide me to my intended destiny.

You don't have to wait for a nervous breakdown like mine to learn to heal your life. You can choose to learn right now, hopefully while you are in a state of joy. If I can inspire you to take the wisdom and lessons these pages contain and not wait for something bad to happen to you to force you to wake you up, then I believe I will have achieved my goal in writing this book.

From the bottom of my heart, thank you for taking the time to read my story. I truly hope you find your gifts and your destiny in the way I have found mine. Don't forget that you are the architect of your life—so design a great one! Inside, you are God, so please never undermine your power to create and manifest. As the Hindu legend pointed out, your power is hidden right inside you. Reclaim it! You can heal your life simply by choosing to connect to a future of hope and gratitude starting right now.

Last, but not least, remember, you are never alone. The Universe is there guiding you, whenever you care to notice. There are miracles waiting to manifest for you. Do the work to be receptive to them. It is worth the effort you make in any measure. You deserve so much more than going through life believing you're the victim of forces outside you. You are not.

Say yes to life and watch your life go from surviving to thriving.

ACKNOWLEDGMENTS

I would like to express my infinite gratitude to Jeffrey, Christine, and my mother for their unconditional presence in my life. To my uncle Marco, for helping always with my translations. To Marla Morrison, for always helping to edit everything I write. And to the rest of my family and friends for their support. I would not be the person that I am today if it wasn't for you all.

To my beautiful daughters, Victoria and Emma, who are the seeds from which my every dream sprouts. Thank you for the love, inspiration, and drive you ignite in my soul.

Special thanks to my spiritual teacher Sabrina Heartsong for her mentoring, guidance, teaching, and inspiration. Thank you for paving the road I so proudly walk on.

Thanks to my editor, Stephanie Gunning, for her guidance in helping shape my dream into the book you are holding.

Last but not least, thank you to my unwavering ally, the Universe, for steering me to my soul's path and for not letting me settle for a life other than the wishes-fulfilled life I deserve.

END NOTES

Preface

Epigraph. Mastin Kipp. *Daily Love: Growing into Grace* (Carlsbad, CA.: Hay House, 2014), p. 63.

1. Omraam Mikhaël Aïvanhov, as cited by Wayne Dyer. *Wishes Fulfilled: Mastering the Art of Manifesting* (Carlsbad, CA.: Hay House, 2012), p. 45.

2. Joe Dispenza. *Understanding the Power of Your Mind* [online course], lesson 4, https://theawareshow.com/store/product/dr-joe-dispenza.

3. Gregg Braden. *Secrets of the Lost Mode of Prayer: The Hidden Power of Beauty, Blessing, Wisdom, and Hurt* (Carlsbad, CA.: Hay House, 2006), p. xviii.

Chapter 1: Roots and Wings

Epigraph. Joel Osteen, Twitter post, December 22, 2012.

Chapter 2: A New Start in a New Land

Epigraph. Alina Ermilova. "Eight Inspiring Quotes to Get You Through the Week," blog post (April 13, 2016), http://www.alinaermilova.com/2016/04/8-inspiring-quotes-to-get-you-through.html.

Chapter 3: A Twisted Turn of Events

Epigraph. William Shakespeare. *As You Like It,* act 2, scene 7.

1. Glennon Doyle Melton. "First the Pain, Then the Rising" [video], *Super Soul Sessions,* Oprah Winfrey Network (May 10, 2017), https://youtu.be/BpBnGHjda14.
2. Marianne Williamson. *Tears to Triumph: The Spiritual Journey from Suffering to Enlightenment* (New York: HarperOne, 2016), p. 54.
3. John. B Goodman. *Moments Matter: Everyday Inspirations from a Soulful CEO* (Chaska, MN.: Goodman Group, 2015), p. 33.

Chapter 4: My Catalyst for Awakening

Epigraph. *The Gospel of Thomas,* translated by Thomas O. Lambdin. Gnostic Society Library/Nag Hammadi Library (accessed May 31, 2018),
http://gnosis.org/naghamm/gthlamb.html.

1. Eric Butterworth. *Discover the Power Within You: A Guide to the Unexplored Depths Within,* reissue (San Francisco, CA.: HarperSanFrancisco, 2000), p. xv.
2. Gregg Braden. *Wired to Thrive: The Six Truths of Extraordinary Living* [online course], lesson 5, https://www.hayhouse.com/wired-to-thrive-online-course-hhu.
3. Joel Osteen. "Message 707: Step into the Unknown," Joel Osteen Ministries (October 16, 2016), https://youtu.be/buXM9maDsEk.
4. Ibid.

5. Ibid.
6. Ibid.
7. Ibid.

Chapter 5: The Best Worst Thing That Ever Happened to Me

Epigraph. Chuck Palahniuk. *Fight Club: A Novel* (New York: W.W. Norton & Company, 2005), p. 141.

1. Viktor E. Frankl. *Man's Search for Meaning* (Boston, MA.: Beacon Press, 2006), p. 67.

2. Marianne Williamson. Facebook post, August 31, 2013.

3. Gregg Braden. "Physics of Our Deepest Connection," *Missing Links,* season 1, episode 6, Gaia, https://www.gaia.com/video/physics-our-deepest-connections.

4. Gabrielle Bernstein. *The Universe Has Your Back: Transform Fear to Faith* (Carlsbad, CA.: Hay House, 2016), p. 19.

5. Frankl, p. x.

6. Wayne Dyer. *Wishes Fulfilled: Mastering the Art of Manifesting* (Carlsbad, CA.: Hay House, 2012), p. 164.

7. Frankl, p. ix.

8. Lisa Nichols, from an interview with Tom Bilyeu. "Never Broke Again," YouTube (November 2, 2017), https://youtu.be/5NsykK5sAWg.

Chapter 6: A String of Miraculous Events

Epigraph. Aletheia Luna, Lonerwolf.com.

1. Nancy Thayer. Brainy Quotes (accessed May 31, 2018), https://www.brainyquote.com/quotes/nancy_thayer_4990 52.

Chapter 7: Being Thankful for the Closed Doors

Epigraph. Gabrielle Bernstein. *The Universe Has Your Back: Transform Fear to Faith* (Carlsbad, CA.: Hay House, 2016), p.138.
1. Joel Osteen. "The God Who Closes Doors" (2016), https://youtu.be/_whc8PoTbnU.

Chapter 8: Giving Time, Time

Epigraph. Gabrielle Bernstein. *The Universe Has Your Back: Transform Fear to Faith* (Carlsbad, CA.: Hay House, 2016), p. 14.
1. Joel Osteen. "The God Who Closes Doors" (2016), https://youtu.be/_whc8PoTbnU.

Chapter 9: Meditation

Epigraph. Lisa Nichols. Facebook post, January 4, 2018.
1. Holy Bible. Job 33: 15–16. Scripture taken from the New King James Version®. Copyright © 1982 by Thomas Nelson. Used by permission. All rights reserved.

Chapter 10: A New World of Discoveries

Epigraph. Joe Dispenza. *Understanding the Power of Your Mind* [online course], lesson 2, https://theawareshow.com/store/product/dr-joe-dispenza.

Chapter 11: Overcoming Early Childhood Conditioning

Epigraph. Earl Nightingale, Brainy Quote (accessed June 14, 2018), https://www.brainyquote.com/quotes/earl_night ingale_390812.

1. Bruce Lipton, as cited by Gregg Braden. *Wired to Thrive: The Six Truths of Extraordinary Living* [online course], lesson 5, https://www.hayhouse.com/wired-to-thrive-online-course-hhu.

2. Bruce Lipton, as featured in *Awake in the Dream*, written and directed by Catharina Roland (Walk on Water Filmproduction, 2013), http://www.awakeinthedream.net.

3. Robert G. Smith, as featured in *E-Motion*, directed by Frazier Bailey (2014), https://www.e-motionthemovie.com.

4. Joe Dispenza. *Redesigning Your Destiny Online Course: Tools to Create a New Life*, lesson 1, https://www.hayhouse.com/redesigning-your-destiny-online-course-hhu.

5. Bradley Nelson, as featured in *E-Motion*.

6. Esther Kochte, as featured in *Awake in the Dream*.

7. Braden.

8. Ibid.

9. From a private conversation. http://www.sabrina heartsong.com.

10. Joe Dispenza. *Understanding the Power of Your Mind* [online course], https://theawareshow.com/store/product/dr-joe-dispenza.

11. Ibid.

12. Marianne Williamson. *Tears to Triumph: The Spiritual Journey from Suffering to Enlightenment* (New York: HarperOne, 2016), p. 157.

Chapter 12: Tapping into the Divine Essence

Epigraph. Wayne Dyer. From a refrigerator magnet.

1. Wayne Dyer. *The Power of Intention: Learning to Co-create Your World Your Way* (Carlsbad, CA.: Hay House, 2004), p. 44.

2. James F. Twyman. *The Moses Code: The Most Powerful Manifestation Tool in the History of the World* (Carlsbad, CA.: Hay House, 2008), p. 16.

3. Ibid., p. 20.

4. Ibid., p. 24.

5. Wayne Dyer. *Wishes Fulfilled: Mastering the Art of Manifesting* (Carlsbad, CA.: Hay House, 2012), p. 46.

6. Twyman, p. 25.

7. Joe Dispenza. *Redesigning Your Destiny Online Course: Tools to Create a New Life,* lesson 1, https://www.hayhouse.com/redesigning-your-destiny-online-course-hhu.

8. Gregg Braden. *Secrets from the Lost Mode of Prayer: The Hidden Power of Beauty, Blessing, Wisdom, and Hurt* (Carlsbad, CA.: Hay House, 2006), p. 16.

9. Ibid., p. 153.

10. Ibid., p. 11.

11. Ibid.

12. Mark Twain. AZ Quotes (accessed June 14, 2018), http://www.azquotes.com/quote/869210.

13. Joe Dispenza. *Understanding the Power of Your Mind* [online course], lesson 3, https://theawareshow.com/store/product/dr-joe-dispenza.

Chapter 13: The Law of Attraction

Epigraph. Kushandwizdom blog,
https://kushandwisdom.tumblr.com.

1. Holy Bible. Romans 4:17. Scripture taken from the New King James Version®. Copyright © 1982 by Thomas Nelson. Used by permission. All rights reserved.

2. Joe Dispenza, *Understanding the Power of Your Mind* [online course], lesson 1, https://theawareshow.com/store/product/dr-joe-dispenza.

3. Ibid.

4. Neville Goddard. *The Power of Awareness: Move from Desire to Wishes Fulfilled* (Camarillo, CA.: DeVorss & Company, 1952), p. 121.

5. Shams-I Tabrizi. Goodreads (accessed June 14, 2018), https://www.goodreads.com/quotes/7577644-when-i-run-after-what-i-think-i-want-my.

Chapter 14: Mindfulness

Epigraph. Joe Dispenza. *You Are the Placebo: Making Your Mind Matter* (Carlsbad, CA.: Hay House, 2014), p. 128.

1. Ibid., p. 110.

2. Joe Dispenza, *Understanding the Power of Your Mind* [online course], lesson 3, https://theawareshow.com/store/product/dr-joe-dispenza.

3. Joe Dispenza. *Redesigning Your Destiny Online Course: Tools to Create a New Life,* lesson 1, https://www.hayhouse.com/redesigning-your-destiny-online-course-hhu.

Chapter 15: Ayahuasca

Epigraph. "Lesson 281," *A Course in Miracles* (Tiburon, CA.: Foundation for Inner Peace, 1977).

1. Darren Weissman, as featured in *E-Motion,* directed by Frazier Bailey (2014), https://www.e-motionthemovie.com.

Chapter 16: Change Your Mind, Heal Your Life

Epigraph. *E-Motion Movie Trailer,* YouTube (posted January 8, 2014), https://youtu.be/uyBZCPrbdpc.

1. Joe Dispenza. "Stay Inspired: Ultimate Truth Is Oneness," *Inspirations,* season 8, episode 5 (March 2016), Gaia, https://www.gaia.com/video/stay-inspired-ultimate-truth-oneness-joe-dispenza.

2. Joe Dispenza. *You Are the Placebo: Making Your Mind Matter* (Carlsbad, CA.: Hay House, 2014), p. 62.

3. Ibid., p. 71.

4. Joe Dispenza, an interview by Ben Fama, Jr. "Conversations of Belief: Joe Dispenza," YouTube (posted December 19, 2017), https://youtu.be/g6raQ8h7Mcc.

5. Joe Dispenza. *Breaking the Habit of Being Yourself: How to Lose Your Mind and Create a New One* (Carlsbad, CA.: Hay House, 2012), p. 281.

6. Gregg Braden. "Physics of Our Deepest Connection," *Missing Links,* season 1, episode 6, Gaia, https://www.gaia.com/video/physics-our-deepest-connections.

7. Wayne Dyer. *Wishes Fulfilled,* Kindle Edition, p. 76.

8. Joe Dispenza, *Understanding the Power of Your Mind* [online course], lesson 1, https://theawareshow.com/store/product/dr-joe-dispenza.

Chapter 17: Gratitude

Epigraph. Michael Beckwith, from an interview with Oprah Winfrey. "The Secret, Manifest My Own Destiny" [video], YouTube (November 13, 2017), http://youtu.be/knzEe6CxKzQ.

1. Joe Dispenza, *Understanding the Power of Your Mind* [online course], lesson 1, https://theawareshow.com/store/product/dr-joe-dispenza.

2. Neale Donald Walsch, featured in *E-motion* [video], written and directed by Frazer Bailey (2014), https://www.e-motionthemovie.com.

3. Joe Dispenza. *Redesigning Your Destiny Online Course: Tools to Create a New Life,* lesson 1, https://www.hayhouse.com/redesigning-your-destiny-online-course-hhu.

4. Gregg Braden, "Our Electromagnetic Heart Affects Reality" [video], YouTube.com (February 15, 2015), http://youtu.be/X1SMgQH7FJU.

5. Gregg Braden. *Wired to Thrive: The Six Truths of Extraordinary Living* [online course], lesson 4, https://www.hayhouse.com/wired-to-thrive-online-course-hhu.

Chapter 18: From Victim to Architect

Epigraph. Jim Rohn, as cited by Asad Meah. "23 of Jim Rohn's Life-changing Quotes," Awaken the Greatness Within (accessed June 14, 2018), http://awakenthegreatnesswithin.com/23-of-jim-rohns-life-changing-quotes.

1. Oprah Winfrey. "Oprah On Forgiveness: This Definition Was 'Bigger Than an Aha Moment' (VIDEO)," Huffington Post (accessed June 14, 2018), https://www.huffingtonpost.com/2013/03/07/oprah-on-forgiveness-how-to-forgive_n_2821736.html.

Afterword

1. Joe Dispenza, *Understanding the Power of Your Mind* [online course], lesson 3, https://theawareshow.com/store/product/dr-joe-dispenza.

RESOURCES

Come to my website:

https://www.waleuskalazo.com

Join me on the social networks:

FACEBOOK:
https://www.facebook.com/waleuska.lazo
TWITTER:
https://mobile.twitter.com/WaleuskaLazo
LINKEDIN:
https://www.linkedin.com/in/waleuska-lazo-337623141/de
INSTAGRAM:
https://www.instagram.com/waleuskalazo

Hire me as a speaker:

Contact Waleuska Lazo at:
Waleuska@dreamcatcherprint.com

Photo by Helen Tansey Photography, Toronto

Waleuska Lazo is a passionate, expressive, engaging entrepreneur, writer, and mother of two with a flair for telling compelling, relevant, and thought-provoking stories. Her writing is raw and healing because it evokes a range of emotions and life-changing behavior in her readers. From her personal journey of self-development has come the mission to help women reclaim their natural power.

Born in Nicaragua, Waleuska immigrated to Canada with her family as a teen. She earned a bachelor's degree and then a master's degree in criminal justice from the University of Toronto. In 1995, Waleuska cofounded Embanet, an e-learning provider of higher education, and sold it in 2007. In 2009, she cofounded the Magnum Opus Group. MOG builds homes for discerning home buyers, homes where dreams are born and legacies are made.

Waleuska's passion for writing led her to establish DreamCatcher Print in 2011. Through its aegis, she has published a series of books for young readers about real-life heroes, which inspire children to lead better lives.

Waleuska Lazo splits her time between homes in Hollywood, Florida, in the United States and Toronto, Ontario, in Canada.

Made in the USA
Coppell, TX
28 August 2020